READ and LEARN™

BIBLE

AMERICAN BIBLE SOCIETY

READ and LEARN™

BIBLE

STORIES FROM THE OLD AND NEW TESTAMENTS

SCHOLASTIC INC.

New York Toronto London Auckland Sydney
Mexico City New Delhi Hong Kong Buenos Aires

ISBN 978-0-439-65126-4

ABS logo trademark and copyright American Bible Society,
1865 Broadway, New York, NY 10023
© Scholastic Inc.

Published by Scholastic Inc. SCHOLASTIC and associated logos are trademarks
and/or registered trademarks of Scholastic Inc. All rights reserved.

19 18 17 16 15 14 13 12   12 13 14 15 16 17 18 19 / 0

Stories retold by Eva Moore
Art by Duendes del Sur
Pencils by Walter Carzon
Color layout by Estela Karczmarczyk
Digital color by Silvana Brys
Revised edition, 2008, book design by make believe ideas, ltd
With special thanks to Claire Page.

Printed and bound at CT Printing in Shenzhen, China, July 2012.
Revised edition, first printing, September 2008

WITH SPECIAL THANKS

Eva Moore is the author of dozens of books for children. Ms. Moore was also an editor at Scholastic for
many years. Her paraphrased retellings of the many favorite Bible stories represented here are beautifully
written and will be an inspiration for children and parents alike.

Dr. Steven Berneking is a biblical scholar and translations officer at the Eugene A. Nida Institute for
Biblical Scholarship. The Nida Institute functions as part of the American Bible Society. It is named after its
founder, Eugene A. Nida, a pioneer in modern biblical translation. Dr. Berneking has helped us in many ways
to ensure the accuracy of these adaptations of the biblical text.

Dr. Richard Bimler has served as president of Wheat Ridge Ministries since 1991. A graduate of Valparaiso
University, he has spent most of his career in the areas of Youth Services and Christian Education. He has
received honorary doctorates from Concordia College in Bronxville, New York, and Concordia University in
Irvine, California. Dr. Bimler is the author of the Parent Pages in this Bible.

WELCOME

TO THE READ AND LEARN BIBLE

The *Read and Learn Bible* is a collection of favorite stories from the Old and New Testaments paraphrased for young readers using the Contemporary English Version (CEV) from the American Bible Society and the King James Version. This introductory Bible for children was undertaken with the cooperation of the American Bible Society, a not-for-profit organization that since 1816 has had the single mission of making the Bible available to as many people as possible so that all may experience its life-changing message.

Combining the American Bible Society's prestige in biblical translation with Scholastic's expertise in early-childhood learning has produced a unique Bible for young readers. It is our goal to make this Bible a new kind of reading and learning experience for children between the ages of five and eight. Not only is the text easy to read and understand, but highlighted information throughout the text brings added meaning and dimension to the stories. In addition, there are supplemental Parent Pages at the back of the book. Dr. Richard Bimler of the Wheat Ridge Foundation has developed these pages. In them, Dr. Bimler explains how parents can share the Bible with their children and help them to understand matters of Christian faith and virtue. Finally, we have brought together a team of excellent artists and designers to make this an exceptionally beautiful illustrated Bible.

OLD TESTAMENT STORIES

THE FIRST SEVEN DAYS
GENESIS 1–2

I n the beginning, God made the heavens and the earth All was dark and empty. So God said, "Let there be light," and there was light. He called the light "day" and the darkness "night." And that was the first day.

Then God said, "Let there be bodies of water and above them a sky." And it was so. That was the second day.

On the third day, God said, "Let dry ground appear." He called the dry ground "land" and the waters He called "seas." And God saw that it was good. He said, "Let plants and trees grow up all over the land. Give them seeds to make more plants and trees." And it was so.

On the fourth day, God made **two great lights**: the larger one to rule the day and the smaller one to rule the night. And He also made the stars. He set them all in the sky to give light to the earth both day and night.

★ TWO GREAT LIGHTS THIS REFERS TO THE SUN AND THE MOON. WE CALL THE LARGER LIGHT THE SUN, AND THE SMALLER LIGHT THE MOON.

Then God said, "Let the waters be filled with fish and let there be birds with wings to fly above the earth." And that was the fifth day.

On the sixth day, God made animals to live on the land.
He made sheep and cattle. He made creatures that move along
the ground. He made wild animals of every size and shape.

And then He said, "Let Us make people in Our likeness,
and let them rule over the fish and the birds and all other
living creatures." So He made man.

God saw all that He had made, and it was very good.

On the seventh day, He rested.

God's Garden

GENESIS 2

God had planted a garden in the east, in Eden. He made all kinds of trees for the garden. The trees were beautiful, and they were full of fruits that were good to eat.

God took the man He had made and put him in the Garden of Eden to look after it. The man was called **Adam**.

In the middle of the garden were two special trees — the Tree of Life and the Tree of Knowledge of Good and Evil.

God said to Adam, "You must not eat the fruit from the Tree of Knowledge of Good and Evil. But you may eat the fruit of any other tree in the garden."

★ ADAM   THE HEBREW WORD FOR ADAM MEANS "OF THE GROUND" OR "FROM THE RED EARTH" AND IS ALSO USED AS A GENERAL WORD FOR "HUMANKIND" OR "PEOPLE."

God saw that it was not good for the man to be alone. He filled the garden with every kind of bird and animal. Adam named them all.

But none of the animals was a good partner for him.
So God made a woman to be Adam's partner and wife.
Adam called her **Eve**.

★ EVE   THE NAME EVE IS THE ENGLISH VERSION OF THE HEBREW
NAME HAVVA, WHICH SOUNDS LIKE THE HEBREW WORD FOR "LIVING."
HAVVA CHANGED INTO THE LATIN FORM EVA, AND THEN EVE, IN ENGLISH.

THE SNAKE IN THE GARDEN

GENESIS 3

Adam and Eve ruled over all the animals in the Garden of Eden.

But the snake was very sneaky. He led Eve to the Tree of Knowledge of Good and Evil. He said to her, "Why don't you **eat the fruit** from this tree?"

Eve said, "God told us not to eat that fruit."

The snake climbed into the tree. "But it is the best fruit of all," he said. "It will make you wise. It won't hurt you."

★ EAT THE FRUIT BY ENCOURAGING THEM TO EAT THE FRUIT, THE SNAKE IS TEMPTING ADAM AND EVE WITH THE DESIRE TO BE LIKE GOD AND KNOW WHAT GOD KNOWS.

The fruit looked so beautiful and delicious. And she wanted to be wise. So Eve ate some. And she gave some to her husband. Adam knew he should not eat it, but he did.

All at once, Adam and Eve felt ashamed. They hid from God.

When God found them, He was sad that they had not obeyed Him. He was angry with the snake for making Eve want the fruit she should not have.

He said to the snake, "Because you did this, you will crawl on your belly and you will eat dirt all the days of your life."

He made Adam and Eve clothes of animal skins to cover themselves. Then He made them leave the garden. God punished them. Life would be hard for Adam and Eve.

God sent angels to guard the gate, and also a sword of fire. No one could ever again enter the Garden of Eden.

The Flood and the Rainbow
Genesis 6 – 9

After Adam and Eve left the Garden of Eden, they had many children. And their children had children. And so it went on for hundreds of years. There came a time when people of the earth did not know about God.

But God could see them. He did not like what He saw. The people were selfish and evil. They fought and did bad things to one another. God was sorry He had ever made men and women to live on the earth. Now He would put an end to all people.

But God wanted to save Noah, because he was a good man.

God came to Noah and spoke to him. "I am going to flood the earth and destroy every living thing on it," he said. "But I want you to build a great **ark** for yourself and your family. Bring into the ark two of every animal, the smallest and the largest, animals that fly and those that walk and crawl on the ground."

★ ARK   THE ARK IS A LARGE BOX OF A BOAT CREATED TO FLOAT, NOT
SAIL. IT WAS HUGE: THREE STORIES HIGH AND THE LENGTH OF ONE AND A
HALF FOOTBALL FIELDS.

Noah built the ark from wood. He made it large enough to hold all the animals and enough food to feed everyone. When the ark was ready, the animals came in two by two.

At last, Noah and his wife and his three sons and their wives went into the ark.

The clouds came and the rain started to fall. It rained and rained.

It rained for forty days and forty nights. The earth was flooded, and every living thing was destroyed. But Noah's ark was well built and floated on the waters. Inside it was dry and warm.

At last it stopped raining, and God remembered Noah.
He sent a great wind, and the water began to go down. After
many days, Noah sent out a dove. When the dove flew back
the second time, it held in its beak a leaf from an olive tree.
Noah knew that the flood waters were going away.

He waited seven more days and sent out the dove again. This time, the dove did not come back. Noah knew that the dove had found dry land to live on. So he opened the ark and let out all the animals.

Then God made a promise to Noah. "I will never again use a flood to destroy life on earth. Life will go on because of you and your family and the animals you took on the ark."

Then a rainbow appeared in the sky. "Look at the rainbow," God said to Noah. "It is a sign of the promise I have made to you."

The Tower of Babel
GENESIS 11

It was a long time after the great flood. There were more people on the earth than ever before. They were like a big family. They all spoke the same language.

The people went east to the land of **Babylon**.

They had an idea. "Let's make a city here. In the city, we will build a tower that will go up to Heaven. We will do it all by ourselves."

The people used bricks and tar. Every day their tower grew taller and taller.

★ BABYLON   THE ANCIENT CITY OF BABYLON WAS LOCATED IN THE COUNTRY NOW CALLED IRAQ. THE NAME OF THE CITY MEANS "GATEWAY OF THE GODS."

God came down to see the city and the tower the people
were building. It was a grand tower, but something was wrong.
The people were working only for themselves. God had to
show them that they would always nccd His help to succeed.

So God gave every person a different language. Now, instead of one word, there were hundreds of different ways to say the same thing. No one could understand anyone else.

The people could not work together anymore. They stopped building the city. The big family split apart and the people settled in different parts of the earth.

The half-built tower stood alone on the empty land. It became known as the **Tower of Babel**.

Babylon was the place where God mixed up the language of the peoples of the earth.

★ TOWER OF BABEL THE WORD "BABEL" COMES FROM THE HEBREW WORD FOR "CONFUSED" (BALAL). IN ENGLISH, "BABBLE" MEANS TO TALK TOO MUCH OR TO MAKE MEANINGLESS SOUND.

ABRAHAM

GENESIS 12 – 17

A braham made his home in a land called Haran. He was a simple man. He lived in a **tent** and tended sheep and cattle.

Abraham believed in God, and God blessed Abraham. God came to Abraham and said, "Leave your country and go to the land I will show you. I will make your name great. All peoples on the earth will be blessed through you."

★ TENT   ABRAHAM LIVED IN A TENT INSTEAD OF A HOUSE. MANY PEOPLE LIVED LIKE THIS SO THAT THEY COULD MOVE THEIR HERDS OF ANIMALS FROM ONE GRAZING LAND TO THE NEXT.

★ ABRAHAM   ABRAHAM MEANS "FATHER OF MANY NATIONS." JEWISH AND MUSLIM PEOPLE BELIEVE THEY ARE DESCENDANTS OF ABRAHAM.

So Abraham left his homeland. He took his wife, **Sarah**, his nephew, Lot, and all of the people in their household. They went from **place to place** with all their animals and belongings.

★ SARAH   THE NAME SARAH MEANS "PRINCESS."

★ PLACE TO PLACE   ABRAHAM COVERED A LOT OF MILES, TRAVELING FROM HIS HOMELAND OF HARAN TO BETHEL IN CANAAN, A JOURNEY OF ABOUT 500 MILES. THEN HE WENT DOWN SOUTH TO EGYPT AND BACK UP NORTH TO BETHEL AGAIN.

Finally, they came to a rich land. But it was not big enough for all the people and animals. So Abraham said to Lot, "Let's part company. If you go left, I'll go right. If you go right, I'll go left."

Lot chose to go east to the rich lands near a big city. Abraham went west to the land of **Canaan**. Here God said to him, "Lift up your eyes and look north and south and east and west. All this land I will one day give to your people. Your children and all who come after will number as many as the stars in the sky."

★ CANAAN   THE LAND OF CANAAN COVERED PRESENT-DAY ISRAEL, THE WEST BANK, THE GAZA STRIP, PLUS ADDITIONAL COASTAL LANDS AND PARTS OF LEBANON AND SYRIA.

So Abraham moved his tents and went to live near the great trees of Mamre at **Hebron**.

★ HEBRON　Hebron was a Canaanite city high up in the hills of Judea, in the Negev (a large dry region) about 20 miles southwest of Jerusalem.

Three Visitors

GENESIS 18 – 21

It was a hot day. Abraham was sitting in the shade of a tree. Suddenly, he saw three men standing nearby. Abraham was happy to have visitors. He welcomed them.

"Let me get you something to eat," Abraham said. He ran to his tent to get food and milk for the visitors. While they ate, he stood near them under a tree.

One of the visitors was God and the other two were His angels. God had chosen Abraham to be the father of a people who would obey God by doing what is right and fair. Now He had come with special news for Abraham.

God said, "I will be back to see you next year. At that time, you and your wife, Sarah, will have a son."

Now, Sarah was standing behind the door of the tent. When she heard the news, she laughed. She was an old woman. Women of her age could not have children. God heard Sarah's laugh. He said to her, "Is anything too hard for God?"

The answer was no. The next year, Sarah and Abraham had a son. They named him **Isaac**.

★ ISAAC SARAH COULD NOT BELIEVE IT WHEN SHE HEARD THAT SHE WAS GOING TO HAVE A BABY AND SHE LAUGHED. HER BABY'S NAME, ISAAC, MEANS "HE LAUGHS."

A BRIDE FOR ISAAC
GENESIS 24

G od blessed Abraham in many ways. Abraham became very rich. He had silver and gold. He had servants. He had many sheep and cattle and **camels** and donkeys. His son, Isaac, grew up to be a strong young man.

Now it was time for Isaac to take a wife.

So Abraham called for his most trusted servant. "I want you to go to my homeland, Haran, and find a wife for Isaac."

He gave the man ten camels. Each one carried bags of gifts to give the family of Isaac's bride.

★ CAMELS   IN THOSE DAYS, PEOPLE OFTEN USED CAMELS TO TRANSPORT GOODS OVER LONG DISTANCES. CAMELS COULD TRAVEL MUCH FARTHER WITH LESS WATER THAN DONKEYS. HORSES WERE NOT NATIVE TO THE REGION.

The servant came to a small town in Abraham's homeland. He led the camels to the **well** in the middle of the town. They were thirsty and tired after the long trip. At the well, the servant saw a beautiful girl carrying a water jar.

The servant said, "Please give me a little water from your jar."

The girl gave him a drink of water. "I will draw water for your camels, too," she said.

★ WELL   YOUNG WOMEN CAME TO THE TOWN'S WELL EVERY EVENING CARRYING THEIR BIG WATER JUGS. THEY DREW WATER FROM THE WELL TO TAKE BACK HOME.

The servant found out that the girl was named Rebekah. And she belonged to the same **clan** as Abraham! This was just what the servant had prayed for. He knew then that God meant for Rebekah to be Isaac's wife. When he told this to Rebekah's family, they asked Rebekah, "Will you go with this man?"

"I will go," she said.

Rebekah left her mother and brother and went with the servant back to Hebron. There she married Isaac, who grew to love her very much.

★ CLAN AT THIS TIME IT WAS TRADITIONAL FOR PEOPLE TO MARRY WITHIN THEIR OWN CLAN. A CLAN WAS DEFINED AS PART OF A TRIBE THAT TRACED ITS DESCENT FROM A COMMON ANCESTOR.

ESAU AND JACOB

GENESIS 25, 27

Isaac and Rebekah prayed that they would have children. They were happy when God gave them twin sons. The first one born was **Esau**. Then came **Jacob**.

★ ESAU AND JACOB   ESAU BECAME THE ANCESTOR OF THE EDOMITE TRIBE AND ALL ITS CLANS. JACOB BECAME THE ANCESTOR OF THE ISRAELITES. GOD LATER CHANGED JACOB'S NAME TO ISRAEL.

The **twins** did not look like each other. They did not act the same. Esau grew up to be a hunter. His skin was ruddy and he had lots of hair on his hands, arms, and neck. Jacob had smooth skin. He was a quiet man who stayed home and farmed the land.

Isaac grew old. He could hardly see anymore. He wanted to give his blessing to his older son. Esau would then become the leader of the people when Isaac died.

But God had told Rebekah that the younger son would be the leader. So she made Jacob dress in Esau's best clothes. Then she put hairy goat skins on Jacob's arms and hands to make them feel like Esau's. When Isaac called for Esau, Rebekah sent Jacob into the tent instead.

★ TWINS   JACOB AND ESAU WERE FRATERNAL TWINS. THIS MEANS THAT THEY WERE BORN AT THE SAME TIME, BUT THEY DID NOT LOOK ALIKE. IDENTICAL TWINS LOOK VERY SIMILAR, EVEN ALIKE.

Isaac knew the smell of Esau's clothes. He touched Jacob's hands and thought they were the hands of Esau. He gave Jacob his blessing and made him the leader of the people of Abraham.

GOD COMES TO JACOB

GENESIS 27–28

When Esau found out that he had lost his place as the next leader of the people, he was very angry. He said that he would kill Jacob.

Rebekah told Jacob he must leave home right away. He must go to live with his uncle in Haran for a while.

And so Jacob left home and went out alone into the desert. He walked all day. When the sun went down, he stopped to sleep.

There was a pile of stones nearby. Jacob took one of the stones and used it as a pillow.

Jacob went to sleep and had a dream. He saw a great **stairway** that went all the way up to Heaven. He saw angels climbing up and down the stairway. And there above them, he saw God.

★ STAIRWAY THE STAIRWAY THAT JACOB SAW IN HIS DREAM IS ALSO KNOWN AS JACOB'S LADDER. THE BOTTOM OF THE STAIRWAY WAS ON EARTH, AND ITS TOP REACHED UP TO HEAVEN.

God spoke to Jacob. "I will give you and all who come after
you the land on which you are lying. I am with you always.
I will watch over you no matter where you go, and one day I
will bring you back to this land."

Jacob woke up and remembered his dream. "How great is this place," he thought. "This is the gate of Heaven."

Jacob took the stone he had dreamed on and set it upright in the sand. He named the place Bethel, which means "the house of God."

Esau Forgives

GENESIS 31–33

J acob lived among his mother's people for many, many years. He had a large family. He had herds of sheep, goats, cattle, donkeys, and camels.

One day, God came to Jacob again and told him to return to the land of his father, Isaac.

Jacob's mother, Rebekah, had died. Jacob had not seen his father in twenty years. He wanted to go back to his old home. But he was afraid to meet his brother. What if Esau was still angry with him?

Jacob had an idea. He called his servants and asked them to take some animals to Esau as a **gift**. There were 220 sheep and 220 goats; there were 30 mother camels and their young; there were 50 cattle and 30 donkeys. Then Jacob went to meet Esau.

★ GIFT   ANIMALS WERE USED AS MONEY AND OFTEN GIVEN AS GIFTS BECAUSE THEY WERE SO IMPORTANT. WITHOUT ANIMALS, FAMILIES HAD NO WAY OF FEEDING THEMSELVES.

What would happen? Would Esau want to fight?

When Esau saw Jacob, he ran to him and put his arms around him. The brothers wept tears of joy.

"Why did you send all these animals?" Esau asked. "I already have plenty."

Each had gone his own way just as God had meant them to. Now God had brought them together again.

A New Name for Jacob

GENESIS 35

Jacob and his family were living in a place called **Schechem**, in the land of Canaan. Then God spoke to Jacob. He told him to go back to Bethel. This was the place where God had first appeared to Jacob.

★ SCHECHEM   A TOWN IN CENTRAL PALESTINE NOW KNOWN AS TELL BALATAN. CANAAN (ALSO CALLED ANCIENT PALESTINE) WAS LOCATED BETWEEN THE RIVER JORDAN, THE DEAD SEA, AND THE MEDITERRANEAN.

Jacob took his family to Bethel. There he built an **altar** to honor God.

Again God blessed the son of Isaac and grandson of Abraham. He said, "Your name is Jacob, but I give you another name. Your name will be **Israel**. You will be the first of a great nation.

And God also said, "The land I gave to Abraham and Isaac I also give to you, and I will give this land to your descendants after you."

Jacob set up a stone pillar at the place where God had talked with him. Then he took his family and moved on from Bethel.

★ ALTAR AN ALTAR IS A PLACE OF SACRIFICE OR WORSHIP. IT COULD BE A SIMPLE PILE OF STONES, OR AN ELABORATE BRONZE TABLE BUILT BY THE ISRAELITES ACCORDING TO GOD'S INSTRUCTIONS TO MOSES.

★ ISRAEL THE GREAT NATION DESCENDED FROM JACOB, OR ISRAEL. ITS PEOPLE WERE KNOWN AS THE ISRAELITES, OR GOD'S CHOSEN PEOPLE.

Joseph the Dreamer

Genesis 37

J acob lived in the land of Canaan. He had twelve sons. The oldest was Reuben. The youngest was Benjamin. Of all his sons, Jacob loved the one named Joseph best of all.

When Joseph was seventeen, Jacob made a fancy coat for him — a coat of many colors. His brothers were very jealous. They could not speak a kind word to Joseph.

One night, Joseph had a strange dream. He and his brothers were out in a field, tying wheat into bundles. His bundle of wheat stood up. Then the others stood around it and bowed down to it.

He told his brothers about the dream. They laughed at the idea that they would ever bow down to him.

Then Joseph had another dream. "Listen," he said to his brothers, "this time I dreamed that the sun and moon and eleven stars were bowing down to me."

Could the dream mean that one day Joseph would rule over his father and mother and all his brothers?

The dreams made the brothers even more bitter toward Joseph.

Sold!

GENESIS 37

"Here comes that dreamer!" Joseph's brothers were out in the fields, looking after the goats and sheep. They saw Joseph coming.

"It's time we taught him a lesson," his brother Levi said. When Joseph reached the camp, the brothers grabbed him. They threw him into a deep pit.

"What should we do with him?" Judah asked.

Just then, some traders came along. They were on their way to Egypt. The brothers sold Joseph to the traders for twenty pieces of silver. But first they tore off Joseph's fancy coat. The traders took him away in chains to be a slave.

When the brothers got back home, they told their father
that Joseph had been killed by a wild animal. They showed
him Joseph's coat, which they had covered with goat's blood.

Jacob wept and tore his clothes. His sons tried to
comfort him. But Jacob would never stop crying for his
beloved Joseph.

JOSEPH AND HIS BROTHERS

GENESIS 39–45

Joseph was not dead — he was alive in Egypt. The traders had sold him to a rich family. Joseph did very well there because God was with him. Joseph lived for many years in Egypt. God gave him success in whatever he did.

In time, Joseph became a powerful man in Egypt, second only to **Pharaoh**, the king.

God had given Joseph the gift of seeing into the future by explaining dreams. Pharaoh had two dreams that worried him. In one dream, seven fat ears of grain were swallowed by seven thin ears of grain. In another, seven fat cows were eaten by seven skinny ones. Joseph said that in seven years, rain would not fall and crops would not grow. There would be a great **famine**. This meant that the people of Egypt had seven years to get ready.

★ PHARAOH PHARAOH WAS THE TITLE GIVEN TO AN ANCIENT EGYPTIAN KING.

★ FAMINE A FAMINE IS A DRASTIC, WIDE-REACHING FOOD SHORTAGE IN WHICH THERE IS NOT ENOUGH FOOD TO KEEP PEOPLE ALIVE. IT IS OFTEN THE RESULT OF BAD WEATHER.

Seven years later, the great famine came.

Because of Joseph, Egypt had food. But people from other lands had none.

One day, a family of brothers from the land of Canaan came before Joseph. They saw a handsome man in fine robes with a gold chain around his neck. They bowed down to him.

The men were Joseph's brothers. The dreams he had when he was seventeen had come true.

When the brothers found out that the great man was their brother Joseph, they were afraid that he would punish them. But Joseph was glad to see them. He said, "Do not be afraid because of what you did to me. It was not you who sent me here, but God."

Joseph sent for his father, Jacob. Jacob and all his sons settled in Egypt, in the land of Goshen. Their children and their children's children numbered as many as the stars in the sky.

The people called themselves Israelites, after the name
God had given Jacob at Bethel.

The Baby in the Basket

Exodus 1–2

F or two hundred years after Joseph died, the Israelites lived well in Egypt. They were called **Hebrews** by the people of Egypt, because they had come from another land.

Then a new king who did not know about Joseph came into power in Egypt. He thought that there were too many Hebrews. He was afraid they would take over the country. So he took away their freedom and made them work as **slaves.**

Their lives were hard, but still the number of Hebrews grew. The king gave another terrible order: All Hebrew baby boys were to be put to death.

★ HEBREWS THE ISRAELITES WERE CALLED HEBREWS WHEN THEY WERE IN EGYPT. THEY CLAIMED DESCENT FROM ABRAHAM, ISAAC, AND JACOB.

★ SLAVES WHEN PEOPLE ARE SLAVES, THEY ARE OWNED BY OTHER PEOPLE AND THEY ARE FORCED TO WORK FOR NO MONEY.

A Hebrew woman named Jochebed had just given birth to a baby boy. She hid her baby to keep him safe. Her daughter, Miriam, and her son Aaron kept the secret.

But the baby got too big to hide. So she placed him in a basket and set the basket in the river **Nile**. The basket floated like a boat down the Nile. Miriam followed it onshore to see where it would go.

The king's daughter was bathing in the river. She saw the basket. The baby inside was crying.

★ NILE THE LONGEST RIVER IN THE WORLD, THE NILE FLOWS ABOUT 4,150 MILES THROUGH EASTERN AFRICA FROM ITS SOURCE IN BURUNDI TO THE DELTA ON THE MEDITERRANEAN SEA.

The princess knew it was a Hebrew baby, but she felt sorry for him.

Miriam saw what had happened. She told the princess she would get a Hebrew woman to nurse the baby. The woman was her mother, Jochebed.

When the boy got older, Jochebed took him back to the king's daughter. He became her son. She named him Moses.

The Burning Bush

Exodus 3

Moses grew up in the palace of Pharaoh, the king of Egypt. He grew to be a strong young man. But **Moses** did not like the way his people were treated.

★ **Moses**   Moses is an Egyptian name that means "is born." He is generally considered the greatest of the Hebrew prophets. He was given God's laws.

He saw Hebrew slaves being beaten and bullied every day.

Moses left the palace. He became a shepherd. He got married and had a family.

One day, Moses was tending his sheep on a mountain. There he saw a strange sight: A bush was on fire, but the fire did not burn the bush!

Moses went up to get a better look. A voice came out of the fire. It was God speaking to him. Moses hid his face because he was afraid to look at God.

God told Moses that He had seen the suffering of the Israelites. He said, "Go to Pharaoh. Tell him I want him to free My people so that you can take them to the land of **milk and honey**, the land I promised to Abraham, Isaac, and Jacob."

Moses didn't think he would be brave enough to face the king alone.

God told him to take his brother, Aaron, with him to speak for him.

"What if Pharaoh does not believe You have sent us?"

God said, "I will give you a sign to show Pharaoh. Is that your staff in your hand? Throw it on the ground."

Moses threw down his staff. It changed into a snake! When he picked up the snake by the tail, it turned back into a staff.

★ MILK AND HONEY MILK AND HONEY WERE IMPORTANT FOODS FOR THE ISRAELITES. THIS PHRASE MEANS THAT THE LAND WOULD BE A GOOD HOME. THEY COULD RAISE GOATS AND BEES, AND THE SOIL WOULD BE GOOD FOR GROWING GRAPEVINES AND DATE TREES, WHOSE SYRUP WAS ALSO CALLED "HONEY" IN HEBREW.

Then Moses went back down the mountain. He and Aaron told the people what God had said. They told everyone to get ready to leave Egypt. Moses would lead them to the land that God had promised.

LET THE PEOPLE GO

EXODUS 5–11

Moses and Aaron went to see Pharaoh.
"Our God has a message for you.
You must free our people and let us go out
from Egypt."

Pharaoh laughed. "I do not know this
Hebrew God. Why should I listen to you?"

"Our God is great," Aaron said. "Look at
what He can do!"

Aaron threw down his **staff** and it became a snake.

Pharaoh had men who could do magic. They did
the same thing. Their staffs became snakes.

But Aaron's staff swallowed their staffs.

Even so, Pharaoh did not believe in God's power.
He would not let the Israelite slaves go. He even treated
them worse than before!

★ STAFF   A STAFF IS A STICK OR ROD USED TO GUIDE SHEEP.
IT WAS ALSO USED TO STEADY A PERSON WHILE WALKING, OR AS A
VERY BASIC WEAPON.

God told Moses and Aaron to go back to Pharaoh. This time, Aaron told the king: "You did not let the people go. Now God will turn the waters of the river Nile to blood."

He put his staff in the river, and the water turned red. There was no water to drink. The fish in the river could not breathe, and they died.

Pharaoh just turned away and went back to his palace. He had seen his magicians do this kind of trick.

But God was not done. He told Moses and Aaron to go back again. They said to Pharaoh, "You did not obey God. For this, your country will suffer a great plague. Frogs will cover the land. They will go into your houses, into your beds, into your ovens. They will be all over you. They will be everywhere."

And so it happened.

This time, Pharaoh did not walk away. He said to Moses,
"Get rid of the frogs! I will let your people go tomorrow."

The next day, the frogs had all died. But Pharaoh changed his mind. He would not let the Israelites go.

Eight times more, God sent terrible **plagues** upon the people of Egypt. Each time, Pharaoh promised to let the Israelites go free if God would end the plague. Each time, God ended the plague, but Pharaoh changed his mind and did not let the people go.

Finally, God said to Moses, "I will bring one more plague on Egypt. After that, Pharaoh will let you go from here."

★ PLAGUES PLAGUES ARE DISEASES OR DISASTERS OF SOME KIND. PEOPLE BELIEVED THAT GOD SENT PLAGUES TO PUNISH EVILDOERS. GOD INFLICTED TEN PLAGUES UPON THE EGYPTIANS.

THE TENTH PLAGUE

EXODUS 11–12

M oses went to see
Pharaoh with a new
message. "God says this to you:
Every firstborn son in Egypt
will die tonight. There will be
great crying and wailing. Only
the Hebrew sons will be spared
because God will protect
the Israelites."

Then Moses left the palace.

Moses told the Israelites to mark their houses with lamb's
blood. Their houses would be **passed over** when the
plague came.

That night, at midnight, the plague came over the land.
All the firstborn sons of Egypt died.

★ PASSED OVER   GOD PASSED OVER THE HOUSES OF THE
ISRAELITES WHEN HE KILLED THE FIRSTBORN OF EGYPT. PASSOVER IS THE
NAME OF THE JEWISH FESTIVAL CELEBRATING GOD'S RESCUE OF HIS PEOPLE.

Pharaoh called for Moses and Aaron. He was broken and sad, for his own firstborn son had died.

"Go!" he said. "Leave my people. Take your flocks and herds and go."

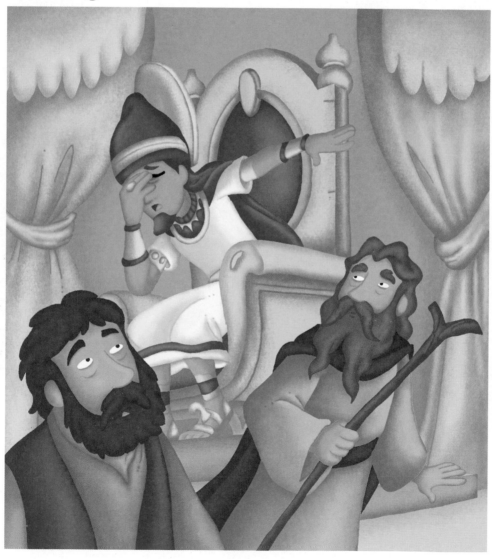

The Israelites left in a hurry. They took pans of bread dough, for they did not have time to add the **yeast** and bake the bread.

On their way, they stopped and asked people to give them clothing and gold and silver. The Egyptians gave the Israelites everything they could. God had put sympathy in their hearts.

★ YEAST   YEAST IS A FUNGUS USED TO MAKE BREAD DOUGH RISE. WHEN THE ISRAELITES LEFT EGYPT IN A HURRY, THEY DIDN'T HAVE TIME TO WAIT FOR THE BREAD TO RISE. THIS IS WHY PEOPLE EAT FLAT BREAD WITHOUT THE YEAST IN IT DURING PASSOVER.

OUT OF EGYPT
EXODUS 13-15

The Israelites hurried along the road. Some led flocks of sheep or goats or herds of cattle. Moses was taking them out of Egypt to a new place all their own. They had to move very quickly.

★ A PILLAR OF CLOUD AND A PILLAR OF FIRE
GOD SHOWED THE ISRAELITES THE WAY BY APPEARING AS A PILLAR OF CLOUD DURING THE DAY AND A PILLAR OF FIRE AT NIGHT. SOMETIMES PEOPLE CARRIED FIRE BEFORE A MARCHING ARMY—SMOKE DURING THE DAY AND THE FIRE'S LIGHT AT NIGHT SHOWED THE WAY TO GO.

God was there to show the Israelites the way. By day, He went ahead of them in **a pillar of cloud**. By night, He went with them in **a pillar of fire** to give them light. And so they could travel by day and by night.

God told Moses to take the people across the desert to the **Red Sea**. When they got to the sea, they looked behind them. A great army was coming!

Pharaoh had once again changed his mind. Now he did not want to lose his slaves. He had sent his soldiers and horsemen to bring them back.

★ RED SEA   THE RED SEA, LITERALLY "SEA OF REEDS," COULD REFER TO THE BITTER LAKES REGION OR THE GULF OF SUEZ, BETWEEN EGYPT AND THE DESERT OF SINAI.

The Israelites had nowhere to run. They cried out in fear. But God came again to Moses. He said, "Lift up your staff and stretch your hand over the sea."

Moses did as he was told. And lo! the waters of the sea divided. Between the two walls of water was dry ground so that the Israelites could cross the sea.

The army of Pharaoh saw what was happening. The
horsemen and the soldiers in their **chariots** rode after the
Israelites into the parted sea. But God slowed them down.
He made the wheels of the chariots fall off and the horses
lose their footing.

★ CHARIOTS A CHARIOT IS A CARRIAGE WITH TWO WHEELS,
PULLED BY ONE OR MORE HORSES. THE CHARIOTS DID NOT CARRY MANY
PEOPLE, BUT MADE IT POSSIBLE FOR PEOPLE TO MOVE QUITE QUICKLY.

All the Israelites passed through the sea. Then God said to Moses, "Lift your hand over the sea once more."

When Moses turned and lifted his hand, the waters of the Red Sea flowed back together. The sea covered the chariots and horsemen. Pharaoh's army was washed away.

The Israelites celebrated their safe journey out of Egypt. All day they sang and danced and praised God. They were free.

Food in the Desert

EXODUS 16–17

The Israelites set up a camp in the desert. As the days went by, the food they had brought with them ran out. Where would they find more food? The people were hungry. They began to complain to Moses and Aaron, their leaders.

Moses asked God for help.

That night, flocks of **quail** appeared all over the camp. The people caught the small birds and roasted them for dinner.

★ QUAIL   QUAIL ARE THE SMALLEST BIRDS IN THE GAME BIRD FAMILY. MANY QUAIL ONLY FLY SHORT DISTANCES BUT THERE ARE SOME BREEDS THAT MIGRATE. TWICE A YEAR, QUAIL MIGRATE ACROSS THE REGION THROUGH WHICH THE ISRAELITES JOURNEYED AT THE TIME OF THE EXODUS. THE QUAIL FLY LOW AND AT NIGHT.

The next morning, there was a layer of dew around the camp. When it was gone, thin flakes like frost were left behind on the sand. Moses told the people, "This is bread that God has given you to eat." They called the bread **"manna."** Manna was white and tasted like wafers made with honey.

Every morning, manna rained down from the sky, so the people always had enough to eat.

★ MANNA   MANNA WAS A FLAKY FOOD THAT APPEARED WITH THE DEW EVERY MORNING, SIX DAYS OF EVERY WEEK FOR 40 YEARS. IT HAD A SWEET TASTE AND COULD BE USED TO MAKE OTHER FOODS.

After a while, the Israelites moved on to another place. Manna still rained from the sky, but here there was no water. The people were thirsty. Again they complained to Moses.

Moses cried out to God, "What am I to do with these people?"

God told Moses to go to a big rock at a place called Horeb.
Moses took with him the staff he had used to divide the
waters of the Red Sea. He touched
the rock, and a stream
of water came out.

The Israelites still
had a long journey
ahead of them. With
manna, quail, and
water, God showed that
He was with them.

God's Laws

EXODUS 19 – 32

It was now three months since the Israelites had escaped from slavery in Egypt. They were camping in the desert of **Sinai** in front of a great mountain.

On the morning of the third day, thunder and lightning filled the sky. A dark cloud covered the mountaintop. Then came a loud trumpet blast that made the people shake with fear.

★ SINAI   THE SINAI DESERT WAS A V-SHAPED REGION OF ROCKY DESERT IN THE SOUTH OF THE SINAI PENINSULA, BETWEEN THE GULF OF SUEZ AND THE GULF OF AQABAH.

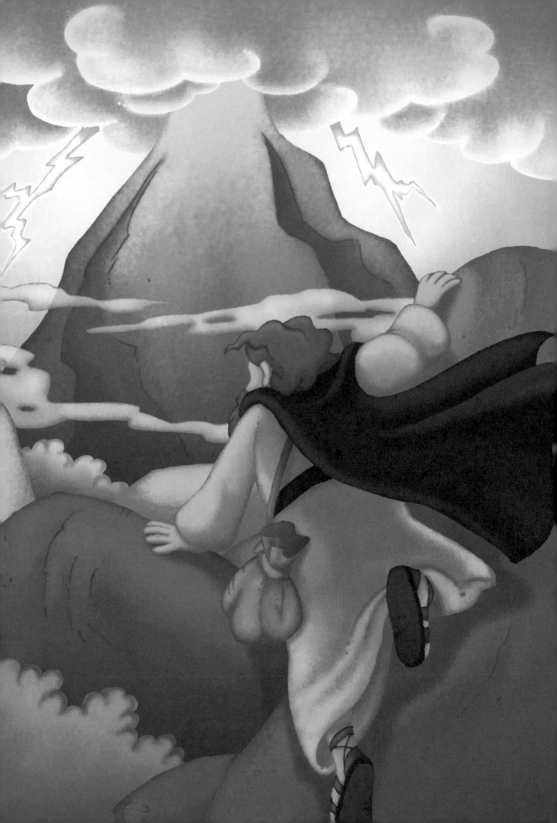

God was in the cloud. He called for Moses to come up to the top of the mountain. There He gave Moses the **laws** He wanted the people to follow.

"I am the Lord your God, who brought you out of Egypt, out of the land of slavery. You shall have no other gods before Me."

"Honor your father and your mother."

"You shall not murder."

"You shall not steal."

God gave Moses many other rules for how the Israelites should behave.

★ LAWS LAWS ARE COMMANDS OR RULES THAT TELL PEOPLE WHAT THEY SHOULD OR SHOULD NOT DO. THE TEN COMMANDMENTS HAVE AN IMPORTANT PLACE IN THE ETHICAL SYSTEMS OF JUDAISM, CHRISTIANITY, AND ISLAM. THE COMMANDMENTS INSTRUCT PEOPLE ABOUT THEIR DUTIES TOWARD GOD, THEIR FAMILY, NEIGHBORS, AND SOCIETY.

Moses was on the mountain for forty days and forty nights. The people started to worry and be afraid. They needed something to make them feel safe.

Aaron told the people to give him the gold earrings they had taken out of Egypt. He melted the jewelry and made a small image of a **calf**. He told them the golden calf was their god who had led them out of Egypt.

Then Moses came down from the mountain. He was carrying two stone **tablets** with God's laws written on them. The people were dancing around the golden calf. When Moses saw this, he exploded in anger. The people were already breaking one of God's laws!

Moses lifted up the stone tablets and threw them to the ground. They broke into pieces. Then he destroyed the golden calf.

★ CALF   A CALF IS A YOUNG BULL OR COW. MANY FALSE RELIGIONS OF CANAAN INVOLVED WORSHIP OF CALF IDOLS.

★ TABLETS   THE TEN COMMANDMENTS WERE WRITTEN ON LARGE, FLAT TABLETS. PEOPLE MADE THE TABLETS OUT OF CLAY AND WOULD WRITE ON BOTH SIDES AND SOMETIMES ALSO ON THE EDGES.

God's Holy Place

Exodus 33–40

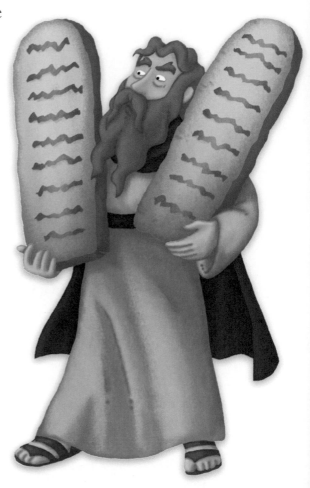

Moses was sorry he had smashed the tablets of God's laws. He went back up the mountain. God said He would forgive the people. He would give the laws to Moses again. He would keep His promise and take the people to the land of milk and honey.

Moses stayed on the mountain for another forty days and forty nights. When he came down, he had the two new tablets of God's laws.

God had told Moses to have the people build a holy place — a **tabernacle** — where they could worship Him.

The people built the tabernacle just as God wanted it. The frames and posts were made of wood from the acacia tree. The tent was made from ram skins dyed red and hides of fine leather. It had a covering of woven goat hair. The linings were made of linen, and blue, purple, and scarlet yarn.

★ TABERNACLE A TABERNACLE IS A PLACE OF WORSHIP. IN THIS CASE IT IS A PORTABLE SANCTUARY IN WHICH THE ISRAELITES CARRIED THE ARK OF THE COVENANT THROUGH THE DESERT.

They made a **wooden box** to hold the tablets of God's laws. It had a special place inside the tabernacle.

★ WOODEN BOX (ARK OF THE COVENANT)
THE ISRAELITES MADE THE BOX OUT OF ACACIA WOOD. IT WAS 45 INCHES LONG, 27 INCHES WIDE, AND 27 INCHES TALL. IT WAS COVERED IN GOLD, BOTH INSIDE AND OUT. IT HELD THE TABLETS CONTAINING THE LAW, WHICH WAS GOD'S AGREEMENT (COVENANT) WITH HIS PEOPLE.

Then God's cloud came over the tabernacle. It stayed with the people on their journey. When the cloud lifted, the people moved. They folded up the tabernacle and took it with them.

When the cloud stopped, the people stopped. They did not set out again until the cloud moved on before them. And so God led them nearer to the land He had promised to Abraham, Isaac, and Jacob many hundreds of years before.

A Big Mistake

NUMBERS 13–14

A t last, the Israelites came to a place near Canaan, the **Promised Land**.

Canaan was a big land with many cities. Each city was ruled by a king. Before Moses could take the people there, he had to find out what it was like. How many people lived there? Were they strong or weak? Was the land good or bad?

Moses chose twelve men to go into Canaan and find out everything they could.

★ PROMISED LAND   THE PROMISED LAND WAS THE
LAND OF CANAAN. GOD PROMISED THIS LAND TO ABRAHAM AND
HIS DESCENDANTS.

Forty days later, the twelve spies came back. "The land is good," they said. "It is rich with milk and honey. But the people are big and strong. Next to them, we felt as small as grasshoppers."

Most of the spies told Moses it would be foolish to enter the land. If there were a battle, they could never win against these giant people. It would be better if they all went back to Egypt.

"No," said Caleb, one of the spies. "Let's go and take the land. I know we can do it." Another spy, **Joshua**, said, "If we obey God, He will surely give us that rich land."

★ JOSHUA   JOSHUA WAS THE SON OF NUN, OF THE TRIBE OF EPHRAIM. HE WAS ONE OF THE SPIES SENT BY MOSES TO EXPLORE THE LAND OF CANAAN. HIS NAME MEANS "THE LORD SAVES."

No one listened to Caleb and Joshua. They turned against Moses and demanded that he take them back to Egypt.

God was angry that the people He had led out of slavery had so little faith in Him. Had they not seen the miracles He could do?

God told Moses that only Caleb and Joshua would get to the land of milk and honey. The rest of the people would have to spend their lives in the desert. After forty years, though, He would take their sons and daughters to the Promised Land.

Into the Promised Land

Joshua 1–6

The time of Moses came to an end. The sons and daughters of the people he had led out of Egypt were grown up. Joshua became their leader.

God said to Joshua, "You must lead these people into the land that I promised Moses I would give you. Do not be afraid, for I will be there to help you."

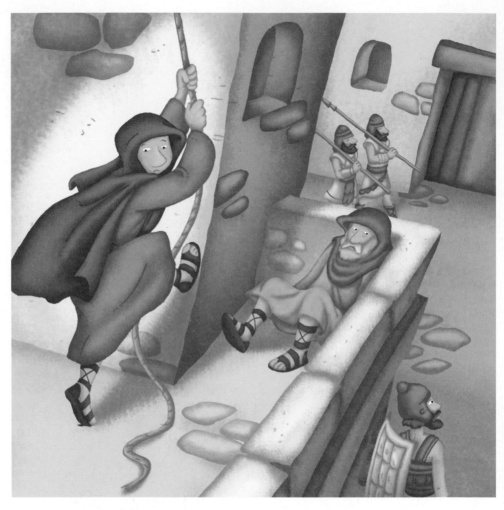

The Israelites were camped along the Jordan River. On the other side of the river was the city of Jericho. Joshua sent two men to explore the city.

The king of Jericho found out about the spies. But a woman named Rahab hid the men on the roof of her house, and the king's men did not catch them.

Rahab told the spies that the people of Jericho were greatly afraid of the Israelites and their God. When Joshua heard this news, he got ready to enter the city.

God told him what to do.

Joshua led his people across the Jordan River. The city was locked tight. No one went out and no one came in.

Joshua sent his army to march around the walls of the city. In the middle of the army were seven priests carrying trumpets.

For six days in a row, the army marched once around the walls of Jericho while the priests blew their trumpets.

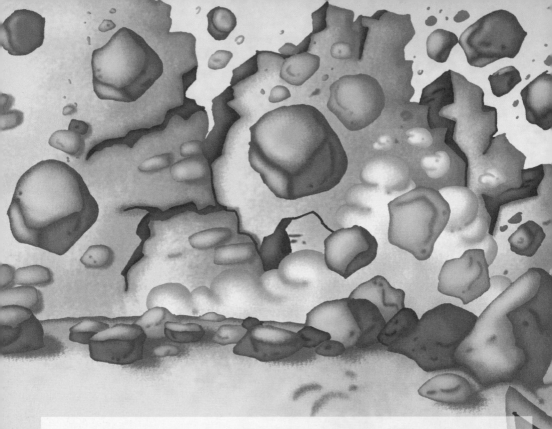

On the seventh day, the army marched around the walls seven times. The last time around, the priests played one loud blast on their trumpets. Then all the soldiers shouted as loudly as they could. At that moment, the walls around the city came tumbling down.

The army charged into Jericho and took the city.

But they did not harm the woman Rahab and her family. This was her reward for helping the spies. She lived among the Israelites from then on.

The Israelites had come to the end of their long journey. No more did manna fall from the sky. The people could now eat food from their own land.

A Brave New Leader

JUDGES 4

I n the years after Joshua, the Israelites settled in many parts of Canaan. But they still did not have all the land that God had promised them.

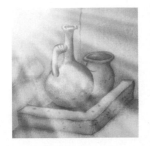

As time went by, they forgot their duty to God. They did not live by the rules He had given to Moses. So God no longer protected them from their enemies.

One of their enemies was **Jabin**, king of Hazor. For twenty years, he treated the Israelites badly. At last, they cried out to God for help.

At that time, their leader was a woman named **Deborah**. God spoke to her.

★ JABIN   JABIN WAS KING OF HAZOR DURING THE TIME OF DEBORAH. IT WAS JABIN'S FORCES UNDER SISERA'S COMMAND THAT WERE DEFEATED BY BARAK.

★ DEBORAH   DEBORAH WAS ONE OF THE FEW WOMEN TO LEAD THE ISRAELITES. SHE WAS ALSO A PROPHET.

One day, Deborah sent for one of the leaders of her army. She said, "Barak, the God of Israel has told me you must form an army of ten thousand men and fight King Jabin."

But Barak was afraid. He said, "I will not go unless you go!"

"All right," Deborah said, "I'll go."

Deborah went to the foot of Mount Tabor with Barak and his army. They faced the enemy. Then Deborah said to Barak, "It's time to attack. God has already gone on ahead to fight for you."

The army charged up the mountain. They fought the army of Jabin. All of Jabin's men fell by the sword. Not a man was left.

Later, Deborah and Barak sang a song about the battle. The song gave thanks to God for leading them to victory against a cruel king.

GIDEON'S ARMY

JUDGES 6 – 8

Some Israelites had settled in a valley that was good for farming.

But they had to share the land with wandering tribes, who moved in with their tents and herds of cattle and sheep.

Once again, the Israelites found themselves in trouble because they had turned from God. The wandering tribes robbed the Israelites and drove them out of their villages. The Israelites had to live in caves in the mountains.

Once again, they called to God for help.

God chose a new leader for His people.

Gideon was a farmer. God came to him and said, "I am giving you the power to save Israel."

★ TRIBES   THESE TRIBES WERE NOMADS CALLED MIDIANITES. NOMADS ARE PEOPLE WITHOUT FIXED HOMES. THEY WANDER FROM PLACE TO PLACE LOOKING FOR GRAZING LAND FOR THEIR HERDS OR FOOD.

"But how can I save Israel?" Gideon asked. "I am not an important man."

"I will help you," God told him.

Gideon was not sure he was actually talking with the God of Israel. But finally he believed. Before long, Gideon had an army of 10,000 men.

"You don't need this many soldiers," God told him. "I'll test them and tell you which ones can go with you."

God told Gideon to take the men down to the spring and ask them to take a drink. Most of the men got down on their knees to drink. But three hundred of them scooped up water in their hands and lapped it with their tongues as dogs do.

This showed that the men were alert and ready for anything. These were the men that Gideon was to choose for his army.

It would be three hundred against many thousands.

At night, Gideon's army surrounded the enemy camp. Gideon gave each man a trumpet and a large clay jar with a burning torch inside. At his signal, the men broke the jars, then blew their horns. The light from the three hundred torches and the noise of the three hundred trumpets scared the enemies. They ran off in all directions and never came back.

As long as Gideon was their leader, the people of Israel lived in peace.

SAMSON

JUDGES 13 – 16

There was a time when the people of Israel lived side by side with a people called the Philistines.

The Philistines were strong. They ruled the land that should have belonged to the Israelites.

God saw that the people of Israel needed a leader who was even stronger than any of the leaders He had sent before.

God sent Samson to lead His people. He gave Samson superhuman strength. Samson would stay strong as long as he did not cut his hair.

Samson let his hair grow and tied it in **seven** braids. He was so strong that he could rip the doors off a city gate and carry them on his shoulders. If someone tried to tie him up, he could break the ropes as if they were mere strings.

⭐ SEVEN THE NUMBER SEVEN STOOD FOR COMPLETENESS OR PERFECTION. ACCORDING TO GENESIS 1: 1–2: 4A, GOD'S CREATION OF THE WORLD TOOK SEVEN DAYS, WITH THE SEVENTH DAY BEING A DAY OF REST.

Time after time, the Philistines tried to capture Samson and put him in jail. Time after time, they failed.

Then Samson met a beautiful woman named Delilah. She pretended to be Samson's friend. But she was really a **spy** for the Philistines. They said they would pay her to find out what made Samson so strong and what could make him weak.

Samson liked Delilah. One day, he told her the secret.

That night, when Samson fell asleep, the Philistines came into the house. One of them cut off Samson's braids. Now Samson was like any other man. It was easy to tie him up and drag him off to jail.

Samson prayed to God to make him strong again.

★ SPY   The Philistines paid Delilah 1,100 pieces of silver to find out what made Samson strong. Samson gave her false answers but eventually told Delilah the truth, and she betrayed him.

At last, Samson had a chance to get back at his enemies. The Philistine leaders took him outside to show him off to their people. Thousands were standing on the roof of a **building**. Samson pushed the pillars that held up the building. The roof came crashing down.

Many Philistines died. So did Samson. He was remembered always as a hero to God's people.

★ BUILDING THE BUILDING SAMSON PULLED DOWN WAS THE TEMPLE OF DAGON. DAGON WAS THE GOD OF GRAIN AND WAS AN IMPORTANT GOD FOR THE PHILISTINES.

Naomi and Ruth

Ruth 1–4

Naomi was an Israelite. She and her husband came from the town of Bethlehem, in the land of Judah. Long ago, they had gone to live in **Moab**. Not many Israelites lived there. After a while, Naomi's husband died. When their two sons grew up, both of them married women from Moab.

Then Naomi's sons died, too. Naomi and her sons' wives, **Ruth** and Orpah, were alone.

Naomi felt lonely. She wanted to go back to Bethlehem to be with her own people again.

★ MOAB   MOAB IS AN AREA ON THE EAST SIDE OF THE DEAD SEA AND WAS NAMED AFTER ONE OF LOT'S SONS. (LOT WAS THE NEPHEW OF ABRAHAM.)

★ RUTH   RUTH WAS THE MOTHER OF OBED, THE GRANDMOTHER OF JESSE, AND THE GREAT-GRANDMOTHER OF DAVID.

Ruth and **Orpah** set out with Naomi along the road to Bethlehem. They had not gone far when Naomi stopped. She told Orpah and Ruth to go back. She knew they could find new husbands in their own land. She wanted them to be happy.

But Ruth loved Naomi as if she were her own mother. She said, "Please don't tell me to leave you and return home. I will go where you go, and I will live where you live. Your people will be my people, your God will be my God."

And so Ruth went to **Bethlehem** with her mother-in-law. They were poor. Ruth picked up bits of wheat from a farmer's field to make their bread.

A farmer, Boaz, noticed Ruth. He thought she was brave to leave her own people and kind to look after her mother-in-law. He grew to love her, even though she was not an Israelite.

Ruth and Boaz got married. They had a baby boy whom they named Obed. Naomi was happy again.

A Prayer Is Answered
1 SAMUEL 1–2

One day, a man and a woman came to the city of **Shiloh**. They came to worship in the Lord's holy tent.

Elkanah and his wife, Hannah, had been married a long time but had no children. Hannah longed to have a baby. At the Lord's tent she prayed to God. Her lips moved but she did not speak aloud. Her eyes filled with tears.

"Lord All-Powerful," she prayed, "please let me have a son. If You do, I will give him to You and he will serve You as long as he lives."

The priest Eli saw that Hannah was acting strangely. Hannah told him she was very troubled and sad. She was praying that God would give her a child. Eli looked at her and said, "Stop worrying. I'm sure the God of Israel will answer your prayer."

★ SHILOH   SHILOH WAS A CITY IN A CENTRAL PART OF CANAAN, WEST OF THE RIVER JORDAN AND SITUATED ABOUT 18 MILES TO THE NORTHEAST OF JERUSALEM.

And so it happened. In time, Hannah had a baby boy. She named him Samuel.

Samuel lived with Hannah and Elkanah for the first few years of his life. Then Hannah kept her promise. She took Samuel to stay with Eli where he could serve God.

God was kind to Hannah. He gave her three more sons and two daughters. And Hannah saw Samuel every year when she went to pray at Shiloh.

SAMUEL THE PROPHET

1 SAMUEL 3

Hannah's son Samuel lived in **the Lord's tent** with the priest **Eli**. Eli was his teacher.

One night, Samuel was asleep. He woke up when he heard someone call his name.

Samuel got up and ran to Eli. He said, "Here I am. What do you want?"

But Eli said, "I didn't call you. Go back to sleep."

★ THE LORD'S TENT ALTHOUGH A TENT, THIS PLACE OF WORSHIP WAS STRONGLY BUILT, WITH DOORS AND DOORPOSTS. IT WAS ALSO KNOWN AS THE TABERNACLE.

★ ELI ELI WAS A DESCENDANT OF AARON, THE BROTHER OF MOSES, WHO HAD LIVED AROUND 300 YEARS EARLIER.

So Samuel went back and lay down. Again, he heard someone call his name. And Samuel got up and went to Eli. "Here I am," he said. "What do you want?"

"Son, I didn't call you," Eli said.

So Samuel went back and lay down.

This happened a third time. Then Eli understood that it was God who was speaking to Samuel. Eli said, "Go back and lie down. If someone speaks to you again, answer, 'I'm listening, Lord. What do You want me to do?'"

Samuel went back and lay down.

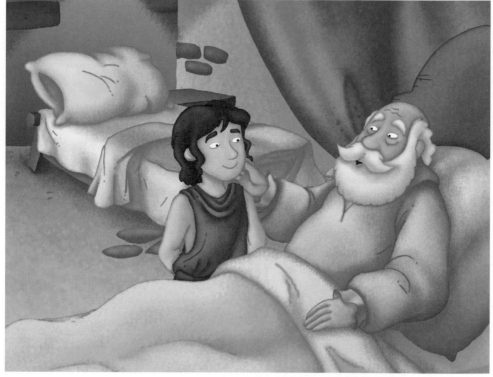

God came and stood beside him and called out as He had done before, "Samuel! Samuel!"

Then Samuel said, "I'm listening. What do You want me to do?" And God spoke to Samuel.

From then on, Samuel was a prophet of God. The people listened to Samuel and he became their leader.

THE FIRST KING

1 SAMUEL 9–15

S amuel grew old. The Israelites began to think about who would be their next leader.

They told Samuel, "We want a king to rule us and lead us in battle, like other nations have. Choose one for us."

Samuel did not like this idea. God was the King of Israel. The people didn't need any other king.

But God told Samuel: "Do what they want. Give them a king."

Now, at this time, the people of Israel were in danger of losing their lands to their enemies, the **Philistines**.

★ PHILISTINES PHILISTIA WAS A COUNTRY ON THE COAST TO THE WEST OF ISRAEL. THE PHILISTINES WERE ORIGINALLY A SEA-FARING PEOPLE. BUT THEY KNEW HOW TO MAKE WEAPONS AND GOODS FROM METAL AND THIS MADE THEM VERY STRONG ECONOMICALLY AND IN BATTLE. THE PHILISTINES WERE THE CONSTANT ENEMIES OF ISRAEL.

God told Samuel He would send him a man who would save the people from the Philistines.

The next day, a striking young man came to Samuel. He was a head taller than anyone else. His name was Saul. He was looking for some donkeys that had run away from his father's farm and gotten lost.

Saul came to Samuel for help. Samuel said to him, "Don't worry about the donkeys. They have already been found."

Saul could not believe he had been chosen to be king. He didn't think he could do the job. But then the Spirit of God went into him and he felt like a different person.

Samuel called all the people together to meet their new king.

But Saul felt shy. He hid among the baggage. Some men went to bring him out. Saul stood before the people.

Samuel said, "Look closely at the man the Lord has chosen! There is no one like him!"

Then the people shouted, "Long live the king!"

A FUTURE KING

1 SAMUEL 16

King Saul had a strong army. He won many battles against the Philistines. But then he stopped obeying God. God did not want Saul to be king any longer.

God told Samuel to go to Bethlehem, to the house of **Jesse**. There he would find a new king.

Jesse had many sons. The oldest one was tall and handsome. He must be the one whom God wants, Samuel thought. But God said, "He isn't the one I've chosen. People judge others by what they look like, but I judge people by what is in their hearts."

The next son was not the one, either. Nor was the next. None of the seven sons whom Jesse brought before Samuel was the right one.

★ JESSE   JESSE WAS THE SON OF OBED, AND THE GRANDSON OF BOAZ AND OF RUTH. HE WAS FROM THE TOWN OF BETHLEHEM. JESSE HAD EIGHT SONS AND TWO DAUGHTERS.

"Do you have any more sons?" Samuel asked.

Jesse answered, "Yes. My youngest son, David, is out taking care of the sheep."

When David came in, God said to Samuel, "He's the one."

Samuel gave David a special blessing. One day, David would be king.

David and Goliath

1 Samuel 17

King Saul's army was in trouble. Their enemies, the Philistines, were camped on a hill across the valley.

The two armies were getting ready for war.

One morning, a huge man came out of the Philistine camp. His name was **Goliath**. He was nine feet tall. He wore a helmet and a coat of **armor** made of heavy bronze. He carried a sword, a spear, and a dagger.

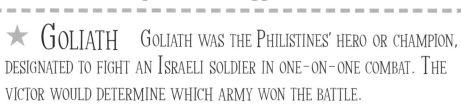

★ GOLIATH Goliath was the Philistines' hero or champion, designated to fight an Israeli soldier in one-on-one combat. The victor would determine which army won the battle.

★ ARMOR Goliath's coat of mail was very heavy, but protected him well and allowed him to move easily.

Goliath stood and shouted to King Saul's men: "Choose your best soldier to come out and fight me. If he wins, our people will be your slaves. But if I win, your people will be our slaves."

No one in Saul's army wanted to fight the giant that day.

So Goliath came back the next day and the day after that. Two times a day, he dared someone to fight him. Day after day, Saul's men ran away.

At this time, David was tending sheep for his father, Jesse. Three of David's brothers were in Saul's army.

Jesse asked David to take some bread to them. While David was at the camp, the giant Goliath came forward.

"Choose someone to fight me!" Goliath called out again. Again, the soldiers of King Saul ran from him.

David said to Saul, "We can't let this Philistine make cowards of us. I will go and fight him."

"But you are only a boy," King Saul said. "How can you fight such a giant?"

David answered, "I have fought lions and bears when they came to take my sheep. The Lord saved me from the claws of the lions and bears, and He will keep me safe from the hands of this Philistine."

"All right, go ahead," said Saul. "I hope the Lord will help you."

Saul dressed David in his own helmet and coat of armor. David could hardly move because he was not used to them. He took them off.

Then David picked up five stones from the stream and put them in his shepherd's bag with his **sling**. With his walking stick in his hand, he stood in front of Goliath.

★ SLING A SLING WAS A BAND OF LEATHER USED AS A WEAPON. TO USE IT, A ROCK WAS PUT ON THE BAND, AND IT WAS THEN SWUNG OVERHEAD. WHEN ONE STRAP WAS RELEASED, THE ROCK WOULD FLY OUT.

The giant jeered at David. "Do you think I'm a dog that you come after me with a stick?" he said.

"You come at me with a sword, a spear, and a dagger," David said. "But I've come out to fight you in the name of the Lord All-Powerful."

David reached into his bag and took out his sling and a stone. He took aim and shot the stone at Goliath. The stone sank into Goliath's forehead, and he fell facedown on the ground, dead.

When the Philistine army saw that their hero was dead, they turned and ran. David had saved the Israelites with a sling and a stone.

DAVID'S FRIEND

1 SAMUEL 18–19

David went to live with King Saul. The king liked to have David sing and play the harp for him.

Everything David did he did well. King Saul saw that people liked him. Saul's son, Jonathan, liked David, too. He and David became best friends.

Soon, King Saul grew jealous of David. He sent him into battle in the hope that he would be killed. But God was with David. He came home a hero.

Now Saul was really angry. **Jonathan** was afraid for **David's** life. He and David made a plan: If Jonathan found out that David was in danger, he would find a way to warn David so he could run away.

One morning, David was hiding in a field behind a large rock. Jonathan came with his bow and arrows. He shot an arrow so it flew far away. Jonathan called his servant boy to run and get the arrow. This was a signal that King Saul was after David.

When the servant boy left, David came out. He bowed down to Jonathan three times. Then they said good-bye. They were both crying, but David cried louder.

Jonathan said to David, "Take care of yourself. Remember, we will always be friends."

★ JONATHAN AND DAVID JONATHAN WAS KING SAUL'S ELDEST SON. WHEN DAVID CAME TO LIVE WITH THEM, JONATHAN BECAME GREAT FRIENDS WITH DAVID AND SHARED ALL HIS POSSESSIONS WITH HIM.

KING DAVID'S SONGS

1 SAMUEL 23; 2 SAMUEL 8
PSALMS 18, 23, 5, 145

King Saul went after David. Three times he sent men to kill him. But God looked after David, and so he escaped Saul's anger.

When King Saul died, David became king. He was a great king. His army

defeated the Philistines and won more land for the people of Israel. He set up a new capital city, **Jerusalem**.

★ JERUSALEM   BEFORE THE ISRAELITES ARRIVED, JERUSALEM WAS AN UNIMPORTANT CITY. DAVID REALIZED IT HAD A SPRING AND COULD EASILY BE DEFENDED. IT WAS ALSO HALFWAY BETWEEN THE NORTHERN AND SOUTHERN TRIBES. DAVID MADE JERUSALEM THE CAPITAL OF HIS UNITED KINGDOM. IT IS STILL SOMETIMES KNOWN AS KING DAVID'S CITY.

With great celebration, King David had the tablets of God's Laws brought to Jerusalem. The people had kept the stones safe since God had given them to Moses. That was almost five hundred years before.

All his life, King David never forgot God. He wrote songs to ask God for His help and to thank God and praise Him. David's songs are called psalms.

David wrote a psalm to thank God for saving him from Saul. This is part of what he wrote:

I love You, Lord God,
and You make me strong.
You are my mighty rock . . .
the rock where I am safe . . .
I prayed and You rescued
me from my enemies . . .
Psalm 18: 1–3

This is part of a psalm David wrote about God's goodness:

You, Lord, are my shepherd.
I will never be in need.
You let me rest in fields
of green grass.
You lead me to streams
of peaceful water . . .
Psalm 23: 12

Some of David's songs are prayers for God's help. One of them begins:

Listen, Lord, as I pray! . . .
You are my King and my God.
Answer my cry for help
because I pray to You.
Each morning, You
listen to my prayer . . .
　　　Psalm 5: 1–3

In many songs, David tells of God's love. This is part of one song:

I will praise You, my God and King . . .
You are . . . always loving.
You are good to everyone,
and You take care of all Your creation . . .
Your kingdom will never end,
and You will rule forever.
　　　Psalm 145: 1, 8–9, 13

A WISE KING

1 KINGS 3 – 4

ing David lived a long life. When he died, his son Solomon became king.

★ KING DAVID   DAVID REIGNED OVER ISRAEL FOR FORTY YEARS. HE WAS SUCCESSFUL IN WAR AND HE UNITED THE NORTHERN AND SOUTHERN TRIBES, MAKING ISRAEL ONE KINGDOM.

Solomon believed in God as his father did before him. One night, God came to Solomon in a dream.

God said, "Ask for anything you want and I will give it to you."

Solomon was just twenty years old. He knew that as king he would have to make many choices. He asked God to make him wise and understanding, so he could make the right choices and be a good ruler.

God was pleased that Solomon had asked for this. He could have asked for a long life, or to be rich.

He told Solomon, "I will make you wiser than anyone who has ever lived."

King Solomon became known for his great wisdom. People came to him from far and wide for help with their problems.

One day, two women came to Solomon. One of the women held a baby. Each woman said that the baby belonged to her. Each said that the other had taken him away.

Which woman was the baby's real mother? Solomon
didn't know.

He had an idea of how to find out the truth. So he said,
"Let's cut the baby in half. That way, each of you can have
part of him."

One of the women said yes; then neither one would have the baby.

But the other woman cried out, "Give the baby to her! Do not kill him!"

Solomon knew that this woman was the real mother. And so he gave the baby back to her.

When people heard the story, they knew their king was the wisest man in the world.

KING SOLOMON'S TEMPLE

1 KINGS 5–8

Four years after he became king, Solomon began to build a great Temple in Jerusalem. His father, David, had dreamed about it long ago.

It took seven years to build Solomon's Temple. The Temple was many stories tall. The outside was made of stone. The inside was made of cedar and pine trimmed with gold and other precious metals.

When the building was finished, the holy box containing the Ten Commandments was taken from the Lord's tent, where it had been since King David's time. The box was carried on long poles to the new Temple. It was placed on a golden altar in a **special room** of its own.

Suddenly, a cloud filled the room. God's glory was in the cloud.

Solomon raised his arms toward Heaven. "Lord God of Israel," he prayed, "no other god in Heaven or on earth is like You."

★ SPECIAL ROOM   THIS SPECIAL ROOM WAS CUBE–SHAPED AND WAS CALLED THE HOLY OF HOLIES. ONLY THE CHIEF PRIEST ENTERED THE ROOM ONCE A YEAR ON THE DAY OF ATONEMENT.

KING SOLOMON'S WISE WORDS

PROVERBS 10, 11, 12, 14, 16, 17, 20, 21

King Solomon had good advice for how people could live a good life and be happy. Here are some of his wise sayings:

Children with good sense make their parents happy, but foolish children make them sad.

You will say the wrong thing if you talk too much, so be sensible and watch what you say.

*Kindness is rewarded—
but if you are cruel, you hurt yourself.*

*Try hard to do right, and you will win friends;
go looking for trouble, and you will find it.*

*Good people are kind to their animals,
but a mean person is cruel.*

*We trap ourselves by telling lies,
but we stay out of trouble by living right.*

It's wrong to hate others,
but God blesses everyone who is kind to
the poor.

Kind words are like honey—
they cheer you up and make you feel strong.

Don't trust violent people.
They will mislead you to do the wrong thing.

Even fools seem smart when they are quiet.

Good people live right,
and God blesses the children who follow their
example.

Hearing and seeing are gifts from the Lord.

The food you get by cheating may taste delicious
but it turns to gravel.

If you try to be kind and good,
you will be blessed with life and goodness and
honor.

Elijah and the Bad King

1 KINGS 12, 17

K ing Saul, King David, and King Solomon had each ruled over the kingdom of Israel.

But when King Solomon died, two men wanted to be the new king. So the country was split into two parts — the north

and the south. The northern part was called Israel. The southern part, where Jerusalem was, was called Judah. Each had its own king.

Some of the kings followed God's laws and treated the people fairly. Others did not.

In the kingdom of Israel, a king named Ahab once ruled.

He said it was all right

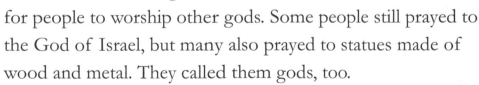

for people to worship other gods. Some people still prayed to the God of Israel, but many also prayed to statues made of wood and metal. They called them gods, too.

One of the false gods was Baal. People believed that Baal caused the sun to shine and the rain to fall. King Ahab built a temple for Baal in his capital city, **Samaria**.

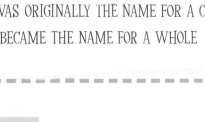

★ SAMARIA SAMARIA WAS ORIGINALLY THE NAME FOR A CITY, WHICH STOOD ON A HILL. IT LATER BECAME THE NAME FOR A WHOLE REGION OF NORTHERN PALESTINE.

This made the God of Israel very angry. He sent His prophet Elijah to see King Ahab.

Elijah said to King Ahab, "So you believe in Baal? I am the servant of the living Lord, the God of Israel. I tell you that it won't rain until I say so. There won't even be any dew on the ground."

And there was no rain that day.

There was no rain that month or in the months after.

But God took care of Elijah. He told him to go to a secret place across the Jordan River. Ravens sent by God brought him bread and meat twice a day. Water flowed in a creek for Elijah to drink.

After a while, all the rivers and creeks in Samaria dried up, and no rain came to fill them.

WHO IS THE TRUE GOD?

1 KINGS 18

For three years, no rain fell in Samaria. All this time, God took care of Elijah. Then God said to him, "Go and see King Ahab again. I will soon make it rain."

When the king saw Elijah, he shouted, "There you are, the biggest troublemaker in Israel!"

"No," said Elijah, "you're the troublemaker. You are not supposed to worship Baal. This is against the Lord's commandments."

Elijah told King Ahab he would prove that the God of Israel was the one true God.

He told the king to call together the prophets of Baal and meet him on the top of Mount Carmel.

Soon a crowd came to see what was going on. Elijah said to the people, "You cannot have it both ways. If the Lord is God, worship Him! But if Baal is God, worship him."

He told the prophets of Baal to build an altar and put wood on it.

He would do the same. "Baal's prophets will pray to their god, and I will pray to the Lord," Elijah told the people. "The one who answers by starting a fire on the altar is God."

Baal's prophets went first. They built their altar and danced around it. They shouted and prayed. But no fire came.

Elijah said, "Maybe your god is daydreaming. Maybe he's on a trip. Or maybe he's asleep."

The prophets shouted louder. Baal did not wake up.

Then it was Elijah's turn. He built his altar with **twelve stones** and placed wood on it. Then he dug a ditch around the altar.

Elijah told the people to pour buckets of water over the altar to make it good and wet. The water filled the ditch.

Elijah was ready. He prayed to God, "Please answer me, so these people will know that You are the Lord God, and their hearts will turn back to You."

★ TWELVE STONES   ELIJAH CHOSE TWELVE STONES—ONE FOR EACH TRIBE OF ISRAEL. HE SAW ISRAEL AS ONE KINGDOM, EVEN THOUGH, AT THIS POINT, IT HAD BEEN DIVIDED INTO TWO.

At that, Elijah's altar burst into flame! The fire burned the wet wood and stones. It burned the ground around the altar and dried up every drop of water in the ditch.

The people all bowed down and cried, "The Lord is God! The Lord is God!"

A few minutes later, the sky filled with clouds. Wind blew, and rain began pouring down.

ELIJAH GOES AWAY
2 KINGS 2

E lijah was the leader of all God's prophets. He did many miracles that showed the power of God. Now Elijah was old and tired.

God sent Elijah a helper, a young man named Elisha. Elisha promised Elijah, "I will stay with you, no matter what."

When God sent Elijah to the city of **Bethel**, Elisha went with him. When God told Elijah to go to Jericho, Elisha went there, too.

★ BETHEL ELIJAH VISITED BETHEL AND JERICHO AND OTHER PLACES TO ENCOURAGE THE LOCAL PROPHETS ONE LAST TIME BEFORE SAYING GOOD-BYE.

One day, Elijah told his helper, "The Lord wants me to go to the **Jordan River**. You must stay here." But Elisha went with him to the river.

When they got there, Elijah took off his coat. He rolled it up and slapped it against the water. At once, a path opened up so the two of them could walk across on dry land. When they got to the other side, the water closed in again.

Elijah turned to Elisha and said, "The Lord will soon take me away. If you are with me when this happens, you will be the one who takes my place as leader of all God's prophets."

★ JORDAN RIVER THE JORDAN RIVER FORMS A NATURAL BOUNDARY BETWEEN ISRAEL AND OTHER NATIONS TO THE EAST. ALONG ITS TWISTING 100-MILE JOURNEY, THE JORDAN DESCENDS FROM 1200 FEET ABOVE SEA LEVEL TO ABOUT 1200 FEET BELOW SEA LEVEL. IT CONNECTS THE SEA OF GALILEE IN THE NORTH TO THE DEAD SEA IN THE SOUTH.

The two men kept on walking and talking. Suddenly, a flaming chariot pulled by fiery horses came in between them. A strong wind blew and took Elijah up, up into Heaven.

"The Lord has taken my master away!" **Elisha** cried. He saw Elijah's coat on the ground. He picked it up and went back to the Jordan River.

"Will the Lord do miracles for me as He did for Elijah?" he wondered.

Elisha slapped the coat against the water. A dry path opened up!

The prophets of Jericho saw what happened. "Elisha now has Elijah's powers," they said. And they made him their leader.

ELISHA'S MIRACLES
2 KINGS 4–5

Elisha followed in the footsteps of his master, Elijah. Many times he showed how strong and good God is.

Once a woman came to Elisha for help. Her husband had died, and the woman needed money to pay his debts. Now a man was coming to collect money that was owed to him. If he didn't get the money, he would take the woman's two sons. They would become his slaves.

Elisha asked the woman, "What do you have in your house?"

"Sir," she answered, "I have only one small bottle of **olive oil**."

Elisha told the woman to go to her neighbors and ask them for their empty jars. She came back with many jars.

Then Elisha told her to pour the olive oil from her bottle into the jars, one at a time.

★ OLIVE OIL   OLIVE OIL WAS VERY VALUABLE. IT WAS USED IN COOKING, MEDICINE, GROOMING, AND RELIGIOUS CEREMONIES. IT WAS ALSO BURNED IN LAMPS.

The woman poured oil into the first jar and filled it up.
She poured again and filled up another jar. With her one
small bottle of oil, she filled up every jar in the house! And
still there was oil left over in her small bottle.

Elisha said, "Now sell the oil and use part of the money to
pay what you owe the man. You and your sons can live
on the rest."

Another time, Elisha helped a brave soldier from another country. His name was **Naaman**. He was very sick with a terrible skin disease.

Naaman heard about this prophet in Israel. Maybe, he thought, Elisha could cure his disease.

★ NAAMAN   NAAMAN WAS A FAMOUS ARMY LEADER FROM ARAM, A VERY LARGE AREA NORTHEAST OF ISRAEL. ARAM WAS NAMED AFTER NOAH'S GRANDSON, WHO FIRST SETTLED THERE WITH HIS FAMILY.

Naaman came all the way from his country to see Elisha. Elisha said, "Go wash seven times in the Jordan River. Then you will be completely cured."

This sounded too easy to Naaman.

If that was all it took to cure him, he could have washed in a river in his own country. But his servants told him he might as well do as the prophet said, since he had come so far.

Naaman walked into the Jordan River. He dunked himself in the water seven times. Right away, his skin became as smooth as a child's. He was cured, just as Elisha had said.

Naaman came out of the river and said, "Now I know that the God of Israel is the only God in the world."

A Lost Book Is Found

2 KINGS 22–23

K ing David and his son, Solomon, were the last kings to rule over all of the Promised Land.

After the land had been split into two parts, their grandsons and great-grandsons ruled in the southern part, called Judah.

Many of the kings of Judah turned from God. They prayed to Baal and other false gods. But not Josiah.

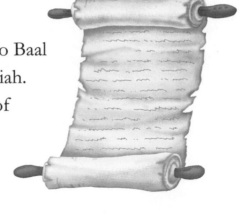

Josiah was the sixteenth king of Judah. He became king when he was just eight years old. As he grew up, Josiah followed the way of his ancestor, King David.

When Josiah was twenty-six years old, he saw that the Temple in Jerusalem was in bad shape. He ordered it repaired. When the workers began to work on the Temple, the king's assistant came to watch. As he was looking through things at the Temple, he found an **old book**. He was very excited.

He brought the book to King Josiah. "Your majesty, look what I found at the Temple!" It was the Book of God's Laws — all the laws that God had given to Moses on Mount Sinai. The book was more than **eight hundred years old**!

★ OLD BOOK   THIS WAS NOT A BOOK AS WE KNOW IT NOW. INSTEAD, THIS BOOK WAS ACTUALLY A SCROLL, A ROLL OF PARCHMENT.

★ 800 YEARS OLD   THIS WAS PROBABLY PART OR ALL OF THE BOOK OF DEUTERONOMY. SOLOMON PLACED A COPY OF THIS BOOK IN THE TEMPLE UPON ITS DEDICATION, 300 YEARS BEFORE JOSIAH'S REIGN.

Josiah read the book. He was upset that the people were not obeying these laws. From then on, he would be sure that the laws were followed.

King Josiah called all the priests and leaders together. He read the book to them. He asked the people to do as the book commanded.

Then Josiah had every statue of a false god destroyed.

No other king before or after Josiah tried as hard as he did to obey the Law of Moses.

A SAD ENDING

2 KINGS 24-25

T hree more kings came after Josiah. All of them went back to the false gods. Finally, God said, "The people of **Judah** have rejected Me. I cannot stand it any longer."

So God let enemies of the people come into the land. At that time, there was a very powerful king named Nebuchadnezzar. He was the king of **Babylonia**.

★ JUDAH   In Babylonia, the Jews were known as the people "from Judah." The Jews spent 70 years as prisoners in Babylonia during the time of Daniel.

★ BABYLONIA   Babylonia was the name for the empire of southern Mesopotamia (or modern-day Iraq).

King Nebuchadnezzar sent his army to Jerusalem. His soldiers went into the city and burned every important building — the king's palace, all the houses, and the Temple that King Solomon had built there.

They tore down parts of the Temple to take back to Babylonia. They took everything made of gold and silver from inside.

And they took the royal family, the leaders of the government, the skilled workers, and the soldiers and led them off to Babylonia. Only the poorest people were left behind to work in the fields.

The people of Judah no longer had a country of their own.

DANIEL AND THE KING'S DREAM

DANIEL 1-2

Thousands of people from Judah were put to work in Babylonia. They were captives. They were not allowed to go back to their homeland.

Three years went by. One day, King Nebuchadnezzar sent for his chief advisor. He asked him to go among the Jews and pick the best-looking, smartest young men. These young men would be taught to speak and write the language of Babylonia. They would be trained to work as officials in the palace.

One of the young men was **Daniel**.

And Daniel followed God's laws. God had made him very wise. He could tell the meaning of dreams.

Daniel was trained for three years. Then the king gave him a job in the royal court.

A few years later, there was some terrible news at the court. The king had given an order that all the **wise men** in the court — including Daniel — were to be put to death.

★ DANIEL DANIEL WAS A MEMBER OF THE ROYAL FAMILY OF JUDAH. DANIEL'S HEBREW NAME MEANS "GOD IS MY JUDGE."

★ WISE MEN THESE MEN WERE MAGICIANS, ENCHANTERS, SORCERERS, AND ASTROLOGERS. THEY MADE THEIR LIVING ON THE ABILITY PEOPLE BELIEVED THEY HAD TO CONTACT THE GODS AND INTERPRET SIGNS.

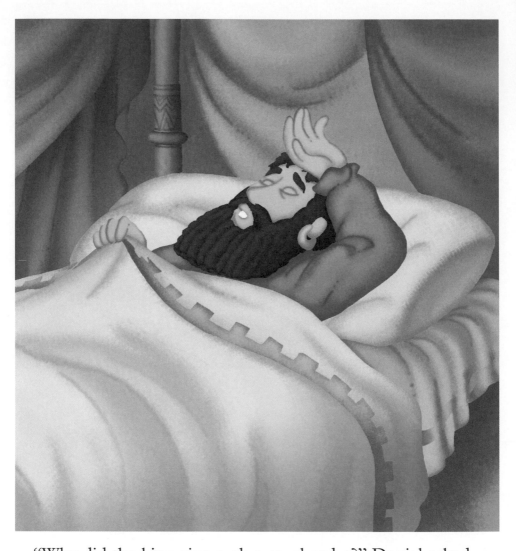

"Why did the king give such a cruel order?" Daniel asked.

The king's official told him, "The king has had a strange dream. He thinks that if the wise men were truly wise, they would be able to tell him about the dream and what it means. But no one can do it, so he is angry with all the wise men."

Daniel prayed to God and asked Him to give him the secret of the king's dream. That night, he saw the dream and its meaning. He hurried to see the king.

"You don't need to put your wise men to death. God has shown me the meaning of your dream," Daniel said. And he told the king what he had seen.

After Daniel had finished speaking, the king bowed low to him. "Now I know that your God is above all other gods and kings because He gave you the power to explain this mystery."

THE KING'S DREAM

DANIEL 2

The king was standing in front of a huge, scary statue. Its head was made of gold. Its chest and arms were made of silver. From its waist to its knees, it was bronze. From its knees to its ankles, it was iron. Its feet were a mixture of iron and clay.

As the king watched, a stone was cut from a mountain — but not by human hands. The stone hit the feet of the statue and broke them. Then the rest of the statue fell and blew away. But the stone grew into a mountain that covered the earth.

Daniel told the king that the dream meant that God had given King Nebuchadnezzar great power. The king was the gold head of the statue. The other parts of the statue were **kingdoms** that would come after him — none of them would be as strong.

But the strongest kingdom of all — one ruled by God from Heaven — would be like the great stone. It would crush the iron, bronze, clay, silver, and gold. It would last forever and never fall.

★ KINGDOMS   THE DIFFERENT PARTS OF THE STATUE REPRESENT:
GOLD—BABYLONIAN EMPIRE
SILVER—MEDIAN-PERSIAN EMPIRE
BRONZE—GREEK EMPIRE
IRON AND CLAY—ROMAN EMPIRE
STONE—GOD'S KINGDOM

THE ANGEL IN THE FIRE

DANIEL 3

Daniel became **governor of a province**.

Once when Daniel was away from the royal court, King Nebuchadnezzar ordered a giant gold statue built. He said it was a great god, and he said that the people should pray to the statue.

There was a big celebration. The people came from far and near to see the statue. The king's servant said, "When you hear the music, you must bow down and pray to the golden god. If you do not, you will burn in a blazing hot furnace."

The music played. All fell to their knees — everyone but three men.

★ **GOVERNOR OF A PROVINCE** DANIEL WAS MADE
THE GOVERNOR OF THE ENTIRE CAPITAL PROVINCE OF BABYLONIA—A
HIGH HONOR FOR A JEW. NORMALLY THIS POST WOULD BE RESERVED FOR
A NATIVE BABYLONIAN NOBLEMAN. DANIEL WENT ON TO SERVE THREE
MORE KINGS OF BABYLONIA AFTER NEBUCHADNEZZAR.

The men were called **Shadrach**, **Meshach**, and **Abednego**. They were Jews and friends of Daniel. "We pray only to the God of Israel," they said. "He will save us from the fire. Even if He doesn't, we still won't worship your gods or the gold statue."

The king was very angry. He told his servants to make the fire seven times hotter than usual. The king's men took hold of Shadrach, Meshach, and Abednego and put them in the middle of the red-hot fire.

The fire did not burn Shadrach, Meshach, and Abednego. The king could see them walking around in the flames. He saw another shape in the fire, too.

The king knew that this must be an angel. He called to them, "You servants of the Most High God, come out at once!"

★ SHADRACH, MESCHACH, ABEDNEGO   THESE WERE THE NAMES KING NEBUCHADNEZZAR GAVE TO DANIEL'S FRIENDS. THEIR HEBREW NAMES WERE HANANIAH, MISHAEL, AND AZARIAH.

The three men walked out of the fire. They looked just the way they had before. The flames had not burned a hair on their heads.

"Praise be to the God of Shadrach, Meshach, and Abednego," the king cried out. "No other god has such great power."

DANIEL AND THE LIONS
DANIEL 6

I n time, the kingdom of Nebuchadnezzar came to an end. Just as the land of Judah had been taken by Nebuchadnezzar, so was Nebuchadnezzar's land of Babylonia taken by the king of **Persia**.

The new king, Darius, divided the country into many states. Each state had a governor. Darius needed someone to rule over all of the governors. He needed a person who was wise and honest. He chose Daniel.

★ PERSIA   PERSIA WAS THE LAND DIRECTLY EAST OF BABYLONIA AND ELAM—MODERN IRAN. THE PERSIANS RULED THE KINGDOM OF BABYLONIA AFTER THE BABYLONIANS, DURING THE JEWISH EXILE, CONQUERING IT IN 539 B.C.

Some other men in the government were jealous of Daniel. They wanted to show the king that Daniel was not fit to rule the kingdom, but they could not find anything wrong with his work.

The jealous men knew that Daniel was a Jew who prayed to God every day. So they came up with a plan to use his faith to get rid of Daniel.

The men went to King Darius. "O King," they said. "You are the greatest king. We wish to honor you. We think the people should honor you, too. Please make a law that says no one in the land may pray to any god or man but you for the next thirty days. If anyone disobeys the law, he should be thrown into a pit filled with lions."

Darius made the law and it was written down.

A few days later, the men came to see the king. They told him that someone in the land was not obeying the new law. The Jew Daniel had been **seen praying** three times a day, even though he knew about the law.

★ SEEN PRAYING DANIEL PRAYED AT AN OPEN WINDOW, FACING IN THE DIRECTION OF JERUSALEM, AS HAD BEEN THE PRACTICE FOR MANY JEWS SINCE THE TIME OF SOLOMON.

Now King Darius saw that the men had tricked him. But the law was in writing, and it could not be undone. Daniel was taken to the pit. "I am sorry," King Darius said. "You have been faithful to your God, and I pray that He will rescue you."

The men threw Daniel into the pit with the hungry lions. The men put a stone over the pit so he could not escape.

All night, Darius worried about Daniel. He could not eat or sleep.

In the morning, he ran to the pit.

"Daniel," he called, "was your God able to save you from the lions?"

From inside the pit, Daniel said, "My God sent an angel to keep the lions from eating me. O King, I have never done anything to hurt you."

The stone was taken away and Daniel came out of the pit. God had saved him because he was faithful and true.

King Darius saw this and ordered his people to honor the God of Daniel.

QUEEN ESTHER

ESTHER 3 – 9

When King Cyrus ruled in Babylonia, things changed for the Jews. Cyrus said that they were free to go back to Jerusalem. But many liked their home and wanted to stay. However, some people didn't want them there.

One man — Haman was his name — did not like the Jews. Haman was a high official in the government of the new king, Xerxes, and he had a grudge against Mordecai, a Jew who would not kneel down to him. This made Haman very angry.

Haman came up with an evil plan that would get rid of not only Mordecai, but all the Jews in the land.

Haman told Xerxes that the Jews did not obey the laws and were a danger to the land. The king believed Haman's lie. He told him to do whatever he wanted with the Jews.

Haman sent out letters in the king's name. The letters said that on the thirteenth day of the **twelfth month**, all Jews in the land could be killed and their money taken.

★ TWELFTH MONTH THE TWELFTH MONTH IN THE JEWISH CALENDAR IS KNOWN AS ADAR. IT IS FEBRUARY OR MARCH OF THE WESTERN CALENDAR.

When the king's wife, Queen Esther, heard about the letters, she was very sad. Mordecai was her cousin. Esther was a Jew herself. She had never told the king.

Should she tell her husband now and beg him to spare the Jews? Or should she stay silent and save her own life?

Esther was beautiful. She was also good and brave. She went to the king and said, "If you care for me and are willing to help, you can save my people." She told him what Haman had done.

The king loved Esther very much. Without a second thought, he made a new law. Now, on the thirteenth day of the twelfth month, the Jews would be able to defend themselves. As for Haman, the king had him hanged that very day.

The Jews survived and had a **big celebration**. They honored the king and their brave Queen Esther.

★ BIG CELEBRATION   THIS IS KNOWN AS PURIM AND FALLS ON 14TH AND 15TH ADAR. ESTHER'S STORY IS READ ALOUD AND WHEN HAMAN'S NAME IS SAID, CHILDREN USE NOISEMAKERS TO DROWN OUT THE SOUND.

Jonah and the Big Fish

JONAH 1–4

O ne day, God came to Jonah in Israel. He told Jonah that he must travel to a distant city called **Nineveh**. The people there were doing evil things. Jonah was to tell them that God was so angry that He was going to destroy them all.

Jonah did not want to go to Nineveh. Those people were enemies of Israel. He wanted nothing to do with them.

Instead, Jonah went to the seaport of **Joppa**. He bought a ticket on a ship that was going far, far away to Spain.

★ NINEVEH   NINEVEH WAS THE CAPITAL CITY OF ASSYRIA, A HATED ENEMY OF ISRAEL. IT HAD 1500 TOWERS AND THE WALLS WERE SO WIDE YOU COULD DRIVE THREE CHARIOTS SIDE BY SIDE.

★ JOPPA   JOPPA WAS A PORT CITY ON THE MEDITERRANEAN COAST OF ISRAEL. TODAY, IT IS KNOWN AS JAFFA.

He was the only Hebrew on the ship.

During the trip, a storm came up. The wind blew and waves came crashing over the ship. The sailors were afraid it would sink.

"This is all your fault," one sailor said to Jonah. "Didn't you tell us that you're running away from your God? Your God must have sent the storm to punish you."

Jonah had a feeling this was so.

"Throw me into the sea," he said to the sailors. "Then the storm will end."

The sailors didn't want to do it, but the storm was getting worse and worse. They threw Jonah into the sea.

At once, the sea calmed down.

Jonah sank down, down into the swirling water. Seaweed wrapped around his head. He knew he was drowning. He remembered God and prayed to Him.

Jonah did not drown in the sea. God sent a big fish to swallow him.

Jonah was safe inside the fish.

He prayed to God. He thanked Him for His **mercy**.

He promised to praise Him and honor Him.

★ MERCY   MERCY MEANS "KINDNESS, UNDESERVED OR UNEXPECTED."
IT IS ALSO USED TO MEAN "FORGIVENESS." MERCY IS A VERY IMPORTANT WORD
IN THE BIBLE BECAUSE IT DESCRIBES THE WAY GOD TREATS ALL PEOPLE.

For three days and three nights, Jonah was inside the fish. Then God commanded the fish to swim to shore. The fish opened its mouth, and Jonah came out.

Again, God asked Jonah to go to Nineveh. This time, Jonah went. He preached to the people about God. They turned from their wicked ways and followed God's laws. God did not destroy them.

PEACE WILL COME

MICAH 4–5

T here once lived in Judah a preacher named **Micah**. God gave Micah the power to see into the future.

Micah saw that the land of Judah was in for trouble. There would be many wars. The army of Judah would be defeated by their enemies.

Micah tried to warn King Jotham. When King Jotham died, he tried to warn the next kings, Ahaz and Hezekiah.

But the kings did not listen. Some of them had turned from God and worshipped false gods instead. Micah said they must obey God, or the people were doomed.

In time, Micah's warnings came true. Judah's enemies destroyed Jerusalem and drove the people from their land.

★ MICAH MICAH LIVED 150 YEARS BEFORE DANIEL AND 100 YEARS AFTER ELIJAH AND ELISHA. HE PROPHESIED THROUGHOUT THE REIGNS OF JOTHAM, AHAZ, AND HEZEKIAH IN THE 8TH CENTURY B.C.

But God had a message of hope for Micah, too. He promised that one day the fighting would end. All the weapons of war would be turned into rakes and shovels.

People would never again make war or attack one another.

A great leader will come, God told Micah. And Micah told the people, "Like a shepherd taking care of his sheep, this leader will care for his people by the power of the Lord, his God. The whole earth will know his true greatness because he will bring peace."

This peacemaker will rule the whole nation. And he will be born in one of the smallest towns of Judah — the town of Bethlehem.

NEW TESTAMENT STORIES

Good News from the Angel Gabriel

LUKE 1: 5–25

When **Herod the Great** was king of the land called Judea, there lived an old man by the name of Zechariah. His wife was Elizabeth. They had no children.

Zechariah and Elizabeth were good people. They tried hard to obey the laws of the Lord God. God saw this, and He was pleased with them.

One day, Zechariah was in the Lord's **Temple**. He was serving as a priest that day.

Suddenly, an angel from the Lord came down and stood near him. Zechariah didn't know what to do.

"Don't be afraid," the angel said. "I am Gabriel, God's servant, and I was sent to tell you good news.

★ HEROD THE GREAT HEROD BECAME KING OF JUDEA, GALILEE, SAMARIA, AND THE AREA EAST OF THE JORDAN RIVER.

★ TEMPLE THE TEMPLE WAS THE MOST IMPORTANT PLACE OF WORSHIP FOR JEWS, AND THE BIGGEST BUILDING IN JERUSALEM. IT WAS 15 STORIES HIGH, MADE OF CREAM-COLORED STONE, AND DECORATED IN GOLD!

"Your wife, Elizabeth, is going to have a son! You will call him John. He will be a great servant to God. Because of him, people who do not obey God will change their ways. John will get people ready for the Lord."

Zechariah was amazed. "But my wife and I are both very old," he said. "How will I know this is going to happen?"

The angel answered, "You do not believe, and so you will not be able to say anything until the child is born."

When Zechariah left the Temple, he could not speak a word. When he wanted to say something, he had to write it on a **writing tablet**.

Soon, Elizabeth discovered she was expecting a baby, just as the angel had promised. She was amazed and happy.

★ WRITING TABLET   A WRITING TABLET WAS A SLAB OF WOOD COATED IN WAX. PEOPLE WROTE ON THEM USING A POINTED STYLUS. THE OTHER END OF THE STYLUS WAS FLAT AND WAS USED FOR ERASING.

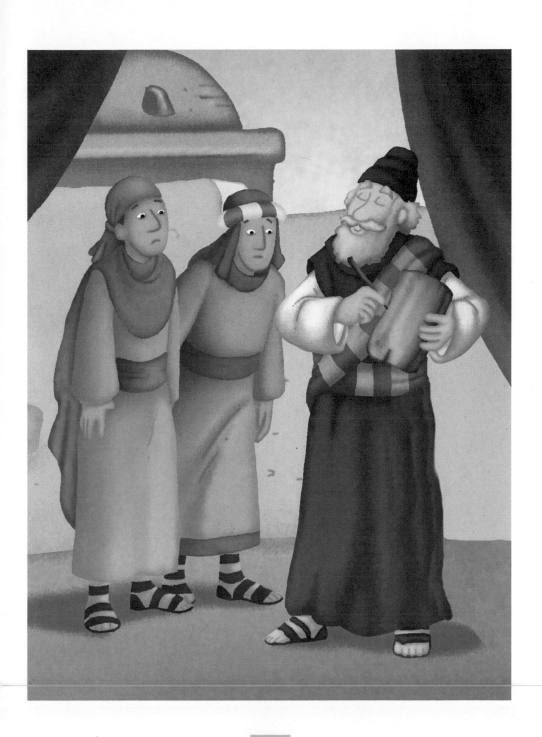

A Message for Mary

Luke 1: 26–55

F our weeks later, God sent Gabriel to the town of Nazareth in **Galilee**.

⭐ Galilee   Galilee was an area directly north of Judea, bordered by the Mediterranean Sea to the west and the River Jordan to the east.

A young woman named Mary lived there. Gabriel had a message for Mary, too. He said to her, "Don't be afraid. God is pleased with you, and you will have a son. His name will be Jesus. He will be great and will be called the Son of God Most High."

Mary did not understand these words. "How can this be?" she asked.

The angel answered, "The Holy Spirit will come down to you, and God's powers will come over you."

Mary put her faith in God. "I am the Lord's servant," she told Gabriel. "Let it happen as you have said."

Mary sang a song to praise God.

*With all my heart I praise the Lord, and I am glad
because of God my **Savior.***

God cares for me.

From now on, all people will say God has blessed me.

★ SAVIOR   A SAVIOR IS A PERSON WHO SAVES OR RESCUES SOMEONE
ELSE, USUALLY FROM DANGER OR DEATH. JESUS WAS CALLED "SAVIOR" BECAUSE
HE CAME TO SAVE PEOPLE FROM THEIR SINS.

A Son for Elizabeth

LUKE 1: 57–80

For many months, Elizabeth's husband, Zechariah, could not talk at all. It was just as the angel Gabriel had said.

Then Elizabeth's baby was born. The people in her family said he should be named Zechariah after his father. But Elizabeth told them, "No! His name is John."

Her relatives couldn't believe it. No one in the family had ever been named John. They asked Zechariah what the baby's name should be.

Zechariah picked up a tablet and wrote, "His name is John."

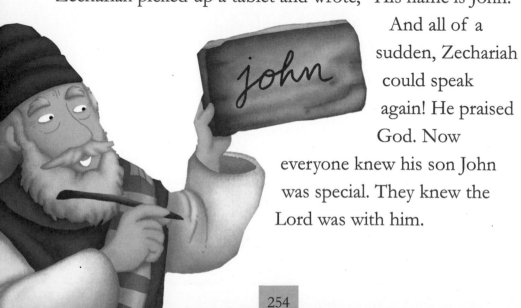

And all of a sudden, Zechariah could speak again! He praised God. Now everyone knew his son John was special. They knew the Lord was with him.

Jesus Is Born

LUKE 2: 1–7; MATTHEW 1: 18–25

It was almost time for Mary's baby to be born. But he would not be born in Nazareth.

Israel was part of the Roman empire. The Roman leader was the emperor **Caesar Augustus**. He wanted all the people in the empire to pay taxes to Rome. But first everyone had to go to their own hometown to be counted.

Mary's husband, Joseph, had to go to **Bethlehem** in Judea. Bethlehem had been King David's home, and Joseph was from David's family.

It was a long journey. After three days, Joseph and Mary came to the city of David. But there was nowhere for them to stay. Finally, a kindly innkeeper allowed them to stay in his barn.

★ CAESAR AUGUSTUS   CAESAR AUGUSTUS WAS THE ROMAN EMPEROR WHO RULED AT THE TIME WHEN JESUS WAS BORN.

★ BETHLEHEM   BETHLEHEM WAS A SMALL TOWN ABOUT 5 MILES SOUTH OF JERUSALEM. IT WAS ABOUT 70 MILES FROM NAZARETH TO BETHLEHEM.

And there in a barn in Bethlehem, Jesus was born. Mary laid him on a bed of hay in a manger.

THE SHEPHERDS

LUKE 2: 8–20

On this night, there were **shepherds** watching their sheep in the fields near Bethlehem.

An angel came down to them from the Lord. The brightness of the Lord's glory shined around them. The shepherds fell to their knees and put their hands over their eyes. They were very frightened.

★ **SHEPHERDS** SHEPHERDS WERE PEOPLE WHO LOOKED AFTER SHEEP OR GOATS. THEY OFTEN WANDERED FROM PLACE TO PLACE, LIVING IN TENTS, AND, SOMETIMES, IN VILLAGES.

But the **angel** said, "Don't be afraid! I have good news for you, which will make everyone happy. This very day in the city of David, a Savior was born for you. He is Christ the Lord. You will know who he is because you will find him lying on a bed of hay."

Suddenly, many other angels came down from Heaven. They said, "Praise God in Heaven! Peace on earth to everyone who pleases God."

The shepherds went to Bethlehem. They found Jesus lying on a bed of hay in a manger. They told Mary and Joseph what the angels had said about their son. Mary thought about this. She wondered what it meant.

As the shepherds went back to their sheep, they could not stop talking about the baby and praising God.

Jesus Is Blessed

Matthew 2: 22–38

Six weeks after Jesus was born in Bethlehem, Mary and Joseph took him to the city of **Jerusalem**. They had to take him to the Temple for a special ceremony. They would promise to bring up Jesus to serve God.

At the Temple, an old man came up to them. His name was Simeon.

God had told Simeon he would see the Savior before he died.

A spirit had sent Simeon to the Temple that day. When he saw the baby Jesus, he took him in his arms and blessed him.

★ **Jerusalem** Jerusalem is the most important city for a Jew. It is also called the Holy City, the City of David, Zion, and Mount Zion.

Then he said to Mary, "This child of yours will cause many people in Israel to fall and others to stand."

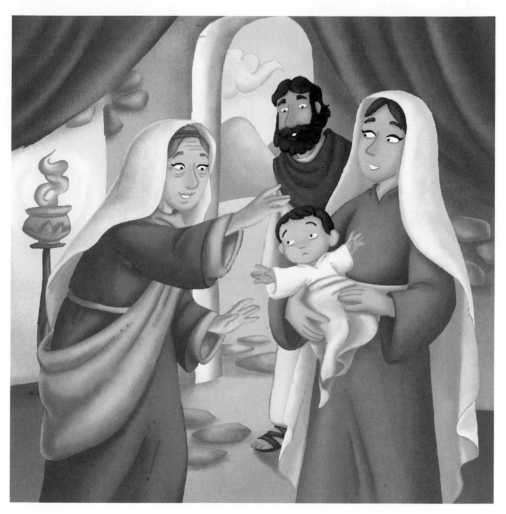

Mary and Joseph were surprised to hear what Simeon had said. They did not understand it.

There was also an old woman named Anne in the Temple. She prayed there night and day. She, too, came to see the baby. She praised God for sending him. She told everyone that the baby would do great things for all the people of Jerusalem.

Wise Men from the East

Matthew 2:1-12

H erod had been named king of Israel by the Roman emperor, Caesar Augustus. Herod lived near the city of Jerusalem.

After Jesus was born, some **wise men** from the east came to see Herod. They asked him, "Where is the child who was born to be king of the Jews? We saw a new star in the east. That means a great new leader has come into the world. We have come to worship him."

Herod was amazed. Could this child be the one the prophet **Micah** had told about? Micah had said that this leader would be born in Bethlehem. Bethlehem was only six miles from Jerusalem.

★ WISE MEN   ALSO KNOWN AS "MAGI," THE WISE MEN WERE PEOPLE WHO STUDIED THE STARS. THEY BELIEVED THAT WHEN A GREAT LEADER WAS ABOUT TO BE BORN, A NEW STAR WOULD APPEAR IN THE SKY.

★ MICAH   MICAH LIVED 700 YEARS BEFORE JESUS. HE PREDICTED THE COMING OF A RULER AND A TIME OF PEACE.

Now Herod was afraid of this newborn king. But he pretended to be glad. He said to the wise men, "Go to Bethlehem and search for the child there. If you find him, let me know. I want to go and worship him, too."

The wise men set out. The star they had seen in the east went on ahead of them. Finally, it stopped over a house in Bethlehem.

The men went into the house and saw the child with Mary. They got down on their knees and worshipped him. They gave him special gifts they had brought with them: precious gold, and the sweet and strong-smelling spices of **frankincense and myrrh**.

Later, the wise men had a dream that told them not to go back to Herod. They went home by another road.

★ FRANKINCENSE AND MYRRH FRANKINCENSE AND MYRRH ARE TYPES OF INCENSE. INCENSE IS A DRY PERFUME MADE FROM TREE SAP. IT PRODUCES A STRONG, PLEASANT SMELL WHEN IT IS BURNED.

THE ESCAPE TO EGYPT
MATTHEW 2: 13-23

After the wise men had gone on their way, Joseph had a dream as he was sleeping. An angel from the Lord came to him and said, "Herod is looking for your child and wants to kill him. Get up! Hurry and take the child and his mother to **Egypt.**"

Joseph got up right away. He took Jesus and Mary to Egypt that very night.

★ EGYPT   EGYPT IS A COUNTRY THAT IS SOUTHWEST OF JUDAH. IT IS ABOUT 100 MILES FROM BETHLEHEM TO EGYPT. IT COULD HAVE TAKEN A WEEK TO WALK THERE!

When Herod found out the wise men had tricked him, he got very angry. He sent his men to Bethlehem with orders to kill every boy who was two years old or younger. Many families lost their precious sons because of the cruel and jealous king.

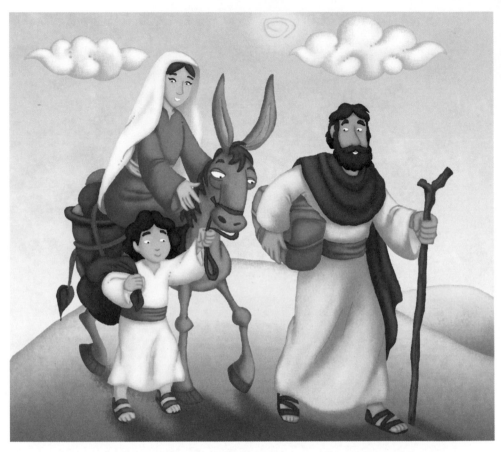

By then, Jesus was safe in Egypt with his parents. They stayed there until Herod was dead. Then God told Joseph to take his son and wife home. They went back to **Nazareth** in the land of Galilee.

★ NAZARETH   NAZARETH IS A TOWN IN THE LOWER PART OF GALILEE. IT IS SOUTH OF CANA AND ABOUT 15 MILES FROM THE SEA OF GALILEE.

Young Jesus in the Temple

Luke 2: 41–52

Jesus lived with his parents in Nazareth.

When he was twelve years old, his parents took Jesus to Jerusalem for the celebration of **Passover**. Every year, the Jews celebrated Passover to remember the time when Moses had led the Israelites out of Egypt, where they had been slaves.

★ Passover   Passover is a very important Jewish festival. It celebrates the night God freed His people from Egypt. By this time, people had been celebrating Passover for over 1,000 years.

After the celebration in Jerusalem, Mary and Joseph left the city to go back home. They thought that Jesus was going back with some other people. But when they looked for him the next day, they could not find him anywhere.

Mary and Joseph turned around and went back to Jerusalem. For three days, they looked for Jesus. Finally, they found him.

Jesus was in the Temple with some **teachers**. He was listening to them and asking questions. The teachers were surprised at how much the boy knew.

★ TEACHERS   TEACHERS TAUGHT THE LAW OF MOSES AND THE TRADITIONS OF THE ELDERS. IT TOOK A LONG TIME TO MASTER ALL THE DETAILS, WHICH IS WHY THEY WERE AMAZED AT HOW MUCH JESUS KNEW.

When his parents saw Jesus, they ran up to him. "Why have you done this to us?" Mary asked. "We have been so worried. We looked for you everywhere."

Jesus answered, "Why did you have to look for me? Didn't you know that I would be in my Father's house?"

Jesus was talking about his Father, God, but his parents didn't understand.

Jesus went back with them to Nazareth. He became wise and grew strong. God was pleased with him.

Jesus and John the Baptist

Luke 3: 1–22, 7: 18–35; Matthew 3: 1–17
Mark 1: 1–12

Y ears went by. Jesus was thirty years old. He lived in Nazareth and worked as a **carpenter**. But his life was about to change. He was about to start the work that he had been born to do.

John, the son of Elizabeth and Zechariah, was thirty years old, too. God's spirit had given him great power.

John lived alone in the desert. His clothes were made of camel's hair, and he wore a strap of leather around his waist as a belt. He ate wild honey and whatever else he could find—even grasshoppers.

Then God told John to go to the valley of the Jordan River and preach to the people.

★ CARPENTER   IN JESUS' TIME, CARPENTERS MADE DOORS AND BEAMS FOR BUILDINGS, AS WELL AS FURNITURE, CARRIAGES, AND FARM TOOLS, ALL FROM WOOD.

John said to the people, "Turn back to God. Come into the river with me. Your **sins** will be washed away and you will be forgiven."

Crowds of people came to the river. John told them that being baptized was not enough. They must do something to show they had really given up their sins. He said they must be honest and fair. They must be kind to the poor.

"If you have two coats," he said, "give one to someone who doesn't have one. If you have food, share it with someone else."

★ SINS   A SIN IS AN ACT OF WRONGDOING; BREAKING GOD'S COMMANDS; DOING WHAT GOD SAYS NOT TO DO. THE BIBLE SAYS EVERYONE HAS A SINFUL NATURE.

Everyone wondered if John could be the Savior they had been waiting for. John told them no. "Someone more powerful than I is going to come. I am not good enough even to untie his sandals. I baptize you with water. But he will baptize you with the Holy Spirit."

John took one person after another into the river. He held their hands and dipped them under the water. While he was **baptizing** people this way, Jesus came. He asked John to baptize him.

John did not think he should do that. "I ought to be baptized by you," he said to Jesus. But Jesus said this is what God wanted them to do.

★ BAPTIZING   BAPTISM IS A WORD THAT MEANS "TO DIP IN WATER."
PEOPLE WERE BAPTIZED TO SHOW THAT THEY WANTED TO STOP SINNING AND
BE MADE CLEAN BY GOD'S FORGIVENESS.

So John baptized Jesus in the Jordan River.

Then Jesus prayed, and the sky opened up. The **Holy Spirit** came down upon him. It looked like a dove. A voice from Heaven said, "You are My own dear Son, and I am pleased with you."

★ HOLY SPIRIT THE HOLY SPIRIT IS GOD'S PRESENCE AT WORK IN THE WORLD. JESUS PROMISED TO SEND THE HOLY SPIRIT TO GUIDE PEOPLE IN THE FULL TRUTH.

TWELVE MEN

MATTHEW 4:18–22, 10:1–4; LUKE 5:1–11, 6:12–16; MARK 1:16–20, 3:13–19

E very place Jesus went, he told the people, "Turn back to God."

One day in Galilee, Jesus was walking along the shore of the **lake**. He saw two brothers. One was Peter and the other was Andrew. They were throwing a big net into the lake to catch fish.

★ LAKE   THIS IS A FRESHWATER LAKE IN THR NORTHERN PART OF GALILEE, KNOWN AS THE SEA OF GALILEE. IT IS SURROUNDED BY CLIFFS AND MOUNTAINS ON THREE SIDES.

Jesus said to them, "Come with me. I will teach you how to bring in people instead of fish."

The two brothers dropped their nets and went with him.

Jesus walked on until he saw James and John, the sons of Zebedee. They were in a boat with their father, mending their nets. Jesus asked them to come with him, too.

Right away, the brothers left their father and went with Jesus.

After a while, Jesus had chosen eight more men to go with him and tell the people about God. Their names were Philip, Bartholomew, Thomas, Matthew, James (the son of Alphaeus), Thaddaeus, Simon, and Judas Iscariot.

The twelve men became his students, his special **disciples**. Jesus taught them everything God wanted them to know.

★ DISCIPLES DISCIPLES ARE FOLLOWERS WHO LEARN FROM A TEACHER. JESUS HAD MANY DISCIPLES. THE MOST FAMOUS WERE THE TWELVE APOSTLES.

A MIRACLE IN CANA

JOHN 2: 1–12

There was a wedding in the village of Cana in Galilee. Mary, the mother of Jesus, went to the wedding. So did Jesus and his disciples.

The party went on for a long time. Then Mary saw that the wine was all gone. She told Jesus.

Jesus saw six large stone **water jars**. He asked the servants to fill the jars up to the top with water.

The servants went back and forth to the well to get water. It took a while to fill the water jars. They held twenty to thirty gallons each.

★ WATER JARS THE WATER IN THESE JARS WAS FOR WASHING HANDS BEFORE EATING. ONE HUNDRED AND TWENTY GALLONS IS ENOUGH TO FILL THREE BATHTUBS!

Then Jesus said, "Take some water and give it to the man in charge." One of the servants dipped a cup into the water and took it to the man.

The man drank from the cup, but it was not water he tasted. It was wine!

He did not know where the wine had come from, but the servants did.

The man called the bridegroom over and said, "This wine is better than the wine we drank earlier. You kept the best until last!"

And so it was in Cana that Jesus showed his **glory**, and his disciples put their faith in him.

★ GLORY   JESUS SHOWED HIS GLORY BY MEANS OF MIRACLES. MIRACLES ARE THINGS THAT ARE DONE TO SHOW GOD'S POWER; THEY ARE ALSO KNOWN AS SIGNS AND WONDERS.

Jesus the Healer

LUKE 4: 38-44

Jesus was living in the town of **Capernaum** near Lake Galilee.

One day, he went to see a friend. The mother of his friend was sick with a high fever. She felt so bad that she couldn't get out of bed.

★ CAPERNAUM   CAPERNAUM WAS AN IMPORTANT ROMAN CITY ON THE NORTH SHORE OF THE SEA OF GALILEE JESUS LIVED HERE WHEN HE WAS OLDER.

Jesus went up to the woman. He told the fever to go away. The next minute, the woman got out of bed. She felt fine. She was able to serve them a meal.

Later that day, after the sun had set, people with all kinds of diseases were brought to Jesus. He put his hands on each person. In that second, the person was well again.

The next morning, Jesus got ready to leave the place. Crowds of people came looking for him. They wanted him to stay. But Jesus said he had to go. "People in other towns must hear the good news about God's kingdom," he said. "That's why I was sent."

JESUS THE TEACHER

MATTHEW 5, 6, 7

M ore and more people heard about Jesus. Soon, great crowds came to hear him speak. They came from places near and places far away.

Jesus and his twelve disciples went up a mountain. Men, women, and children followed them. Jesus sat on the side of the mountain and the people sat below him. He had many lessons to teach them.

THE BEATITUDES

"God blesses all who depend only on Him. They belong to the Kingdom of Heaven."

"God blesses all who feel sadness. They will find comfort."

"God blesses all who are humble, who do not boast and brag. The earth will belong to them."

★ THE BEATITUDES   These sayings are known as the Beatitudes. The Latin word "beatitudo" means "supremely blessed," or "happy." When God blesses people it means God is pleased with them. People who are blessed gain happiness from the knowledge that they are pleasing God.

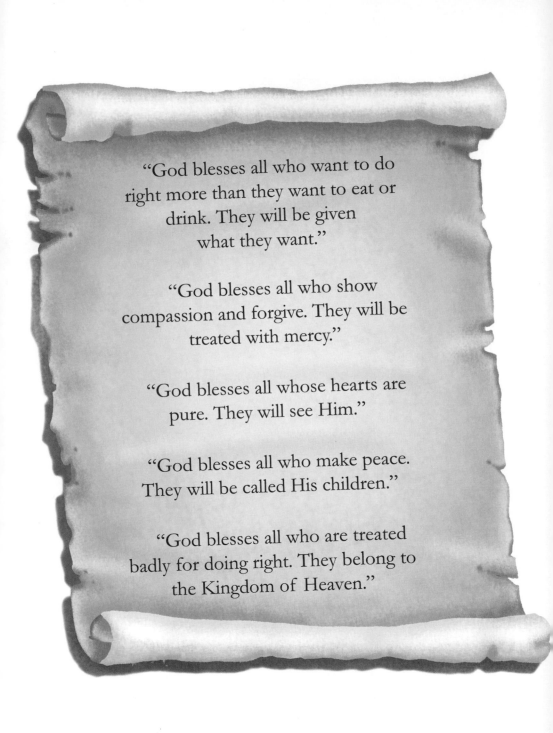

"God blesses all who want to do right more than they want to eat or drink. They will be given what they want."

"God blesses all who show compassion and forgive. They will be treated with mercy."

"God blesses all whose hearts are pure. They will see Him."

"God blesses all who make peace. They will be called His children."

"God blesses all who are treated badly for doing right. They belong to the Kingdom of Heaven."

SOME WORDS OF JESUS

reat others as you want them to treat you. This is what the **Law** and the **Prophets** are all about."

"When you do good deeds, don't try to show off. When you give to the poor, don't blow a loud horn. Then your gift

★ LAW   THE LAW IS MADE UP OF THE FIVE BOOKS OF MOSES. THEY CONTAIN GOD'S MOST IMPORTANT INSTRUCTIONS TO HIS PEOPLE.

★ PROPHETS   THESE ARE THE OLD TESTAMENT BOOKS THAT RECORD THE TEACHINGS GIVEN BY A NUMBER OF PROPHETS BETWEEN 900 AND 500 B.C.

will be given in secret. Your Father knows what is done in secret, and He will reward you."

"Ask, and you will receive. Search, and you will find. Knock, and the door will be opened for you. Everyone who asks will receive. Everyone who searches will find. And the door will be opened for everyone who knocks."

"Watch out for **false prophets**! They dress up like sheep, but inside they are wolves who have come to attack you. You can tell what they are by what they do."

★ FALSE PROPHETS FALSE PROPHETS ARE PEOPLE WHO CLAIM TO SPEAK FOR GOD WHEN REALLY THEY DO NOT. JESUS TELLS US TO LOOK AT WHAT PEOPLE DO RATHER THAN WHAT THEY SAY.

"You are like light for the whole world. No one would light a lamp and put it under a clay pot. A lamp is placed where it can give light to everyone in the house. Make your light shine, so that others will see the good you do and will praise your Father in Heaven."

THE LORD'S PRAYER
MATTHEW 6: 5-13

Go into a room alone and close the door. Pray to your Father in private. He knows what is done in private, and He will reward you.

When you pray, don't go on and on. Your Father knows what you need before you ask.

You should pray like this:

*Our Father in **Heaven**, help us to **honor** Your name. Come and set up Your kingdom, so that everyone on earth will obey You, as You are obeyed in Heaven. Give us our food for today. Forgive us for doing wrong, as we forgive others. Keep us from being tempted and protect us from evil.*

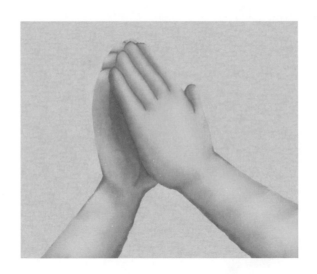

★ HEAVEN   HEAVEN IS GOD'S HOME AND THE HOME OF ALL THOSE WHO LOVE HIM. THE ANGELS LIVE IN HEAVEN WITH GOD. JESUS PROMISED TO PREPARE A PLACE FOR HIS PEOPLE IN HEAVEN.

★ HONOR   WHEN YOU HONOR PEOPLE, YOU SHOW GREAT RESPECT FOR THEM. THE WORD "HALLOWED" MEANS TO "HONOR SOMEONE HOLY."

JESUS AND THE ROMAN SOLDIER

MATTHEW 8: 5–13; LUKE 7: 1–10

A t the time Jesus lived, the people in Galilee and all the other regions of Israel were part of the huge

Roman Empire. The emperor of Rome had placed soldiers in every town and village.

One day when Jesus was in the town of Capernaum, an army officer from Rome came up to him. As usual, Jesus was surrounded by a crowd of people. The soldier said, "Lord, my servant is at home in terrible pain. He is very sick. I'm afraid he will die."

"I will go and heal him," Jesus said.

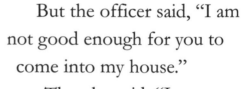

But the officer said, "I am not good enough for you to come into my house."

Then he said, "I am an officer. I have soldiers who take orders from me. If I say, 'Go,' the soldier will go. If I say, 'Come,' he comes. I can say to my servant, 'Do this,' and he will do it. I know that all you have to do is say the word and my servant will get well."

★ ROMAN EMPIRE ROME IS THE CAPITAL OF ITALY. IN JESUS' TIME, THE ROMANS INVADED COUNTRIES AND RULED THEM SO THAT THE EMPIRE STRETCHED FROM BRITAIN TO NORTH AFRICA AND PALESTINE.

Jesus was surprised by what the officer had said. He turned
to the people who had been following him. "In all of Israel
I've never found anyone with this much faith!" he said.

Then he said to the officer, "Go home now. Your **faith** has made it happen."

When the officer returned home, he found that his servant was healed. It had happened just as Jesus had said.

★ FAITH   WHEN YOU HAVE FAITH, YOU PUT YOUR TRUST IN GOD. YOU DO NOT HAVE TO WAIT TO SEE SOMETHING HAPPEN, BUT YOU BELIEVE THAT IT WILL HAPPEN.

A Storm

LUKE 8: 22–25; MATTHEW 8: 23–27; MARK 4: 35–41

One day in Galilee, Jesus and his disciples wanted to cross the lake. They got into a boat.

The lake was very big. When they got to the middle, dark clouds came up and the wind started to blow. The waves in the lake splashed up into the boat.

Jesus was in the back of the boat with his head on a pillow. He was asleep. The disciples woke him up. "Teacher, teacher," they said. "We are about to drown!"

Jesus got up. He told the wind and the waves to be quiet. Then everything was calm.

Jesus asked his disciples, "Why were you afraid? Don't you have any faith?"

The men in the boat were amazed. "Who is this?" they asked one another. "Even the wind and the waves obey him!"

Jesus Heals a Crippled Man

MARK 2: 1–12; LUKE 5: 17–26; MATTHEW 9: 1–8

Everywhere Jesus went, people came to see him.

Once, Jesus was teaching to a large crowd of people in a house in Capernaum. Four people came carrying a man on a mat. The man's legs were twisted. He could not walk. His friends had heard that Jesus had the power to heal the sick. They had brought their friend to be healed.

But people were crowded around the door. The men could not get in.

In those days, most houses had stairs on the outside that went up to the roof. The men carried their friend up the stairs. They took some tiles off the roof and made a big opening. Then they lowered the mat down to the middle of the room where Jesus stood.

Jesus saw how much faith the friends had. He said to the crippled man, "My friend, your sins are **forgiven**."

This upset some people in the crowd. They thought he must think he is God! Only God can forgive sins.

Jesus knew what they were thinking. He said to them, "Is it easier for me to tell this crippled man that his sins are forgiven, or to tell him to get up and walk? I will show you that I have the right to forgive sins here on earth."

So Jesus looked at the man and said, "Get up! Pick up your mat and go on home."

★ FORGIVEN   WHEN SINS ARE FORGIVEN, A PERSON IS PARDONED OR SET FREE FROM THEM. PEOPLE CAN ALSO FORGIVE, OR CANCEL, SOMEONE ELSE'S DEBT.

The man got right up. He picked up his mat and left.
Everyone was amazed. They praised God and said, "We
have seen a great miracle today."

Two Miracles in One Day

MARK 5: 21 – 43; LUKE 8: 40 – 56; MATTHEW 9: 18 – 26

People came running to Lake Galilee. Jesus had just gotten out of a boat and was standing on the shore.

A man broke through the crowd. His name was Jairus. He fell to his knees in front of Jesus.

"Help me," he begged. "My daughter is about to die! Please come and touch her, so she will get well and live."

Jesus went with Jairus. The people pressed in around them. A woman who was right behind Jesus reached out and gently touched his clothes.

The woman had been sick for twelve years. She had spent all her money on doctors, but no one could cure her. She believed that if she could only touch Jesus' clothes, she would be well.

Jesus felt a tug on his clothes. He turned around and saw the woman.

He said to her, "You are now well because of your faith. May God give you peace."

Jesus went on to the house where Jairus' daughter was.
The people inside were crying. They said the girl was
already dead.

Jesus said to them, "The child isn't dead. She is just
asleep." He went to the girl's bed and took hold of her hand.
He said, "Little girl, get up!"

The girl got right up and started walking around.
Everyone was surprised.
Then Jesus said, "Give her something to eat."
She **ate**, and they knew she was not a ghost. She really was alive.

★ ATE WHEN SOMEONE EATS, IT IS A SIGN THAT THEY ARE ALIVE. GHOSTS DO NOT EAT, SINCE THEY DO NOT NEED FOOD TO SURVIVE.

Women Helpers

LUKE 8: 1–3

J esus had been preaching in towns around Lake Galilee. Now he and his disciples began to go out to other places farther away. They went to villages all over

Galilee telling the good news about **God's kingdom**.

They had no worldly goods and never asked anyone for money. But people gave them money and helped them because they believed in Jesus.

Some of these **helpers** were women Jesus had cured of all kinds of terrible sickness. The women traveled with him from town to town.

Three of the women were Joanna, Susanna, and Mary Magdalene. Their lives had been changed by Jesus. Now they wanted to help Jesus if they could.

★ GOD'S KINGDOM   OTHER KINGDOMS OR COUNTRIES HAVE GEOGRAPHICAL BORDERS AND CAN BE SHOWN ON A MAP, BUT GOD'S KINGDOM EXISTS IN PEOPLE'S HEARTS, WHERE GOD RULES.

★ HELPERS   PEOPLE PROVIDED MONEY AND GOODS FOR TEACHERS WHO TRAVELED FROM TOWN TO TOWN.

But best of all was their faith in Jesus. The women helped to show people how good he was and how great was the promise of the kingdom of God.

A Very
Important Story
MATTHEW 13: 1–9, 18–23; MARK 4: 1–9, 13–20; LUKE 8: 4–8, 11–15

J esus taught his followers by telling stories.

One day he was at Lake Galilee. People came to hear him talk. There were so many people on the lakeshore that there was no room for Jesus. He had to go out onto a **boat**. He sat in the boat and told the people this story:

"A farmer went out to a field to plant seeds. On his way, some seeds fell out onto the road.

"These seeds were stepped on or eaten by birds.

"Other seeds fell on rocky ground where there was not much soil. Some of these seeds started growing, but the plants could not get enough **water** and soon dried up.

★ WATER   In Israel, the summer is long, very hot, and dry. The winter is short, warm, and rainy. As you go south, the rainfall gets less and less.

"Some other seeds fell where thornbushes grew. These bushes were so thick and prickly that there was no room for new plants to grow.

"The rest of the seeds fell on good ground. Plants grew from these seeds and made more seeds. They produced a hundred times as many seeds as the farmer planted."

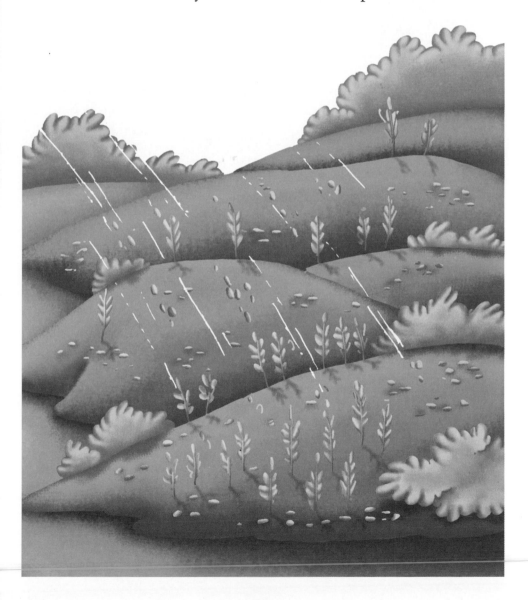

Jesus then said, "This is what the story means:

"The farmer is really planting a message about God's kingdom. The seeds that fell along the road are the people who hear the message. But the **devil** comes along and takes it away from them, so they will not **believe** and be saved.

★ DEVIL THE DEVIL, ALSO KNOWN AS SATAN, IS GOD'S ENEMY AND TRIES TO STOP GOD'S WORK IN THE WORLD.

★ BELIEVE WHEN YOU BELIEVE SOMETHING, YOU ACCEPT THAT IT IS TRUE AND YOU HAVE CONFIDENCE IN IT. YOU DO NOT HAVE TO HAVE PROOF TO KNOW THAT IT IS TRUE.

"The seeds that fell on rocky ground are the people who hear the message and accept it right away. But they don't have deep roots, so they believe only for a little while. As soon as life gets hard, they give up.

"The seeds that fell among the thornbushes are also people who hear the message. But they start worrying about the things they need in life and how to get rich. So there is no room for the message to get through.

"The seeds that fell on good ground are the people who listen to the message and keep it in good and honest hearts. They last and produce enough plants for a good harvest."

THE KINGDOM OF HEAVEN

MATTHEW 13: 44-50

A fter the people left, Jesus stayed in the boat. He told his twelve disciples some stories about the Kingdom of Heaven.

He said, "The Kingdom of Heaven is like what happens when someone finds a treasure hidden in a field and buries it again. A person like that is happy and goes and sells everything in order to buy that field.

"The Kingdom of Heaven is like what happens when a shop owner is looking for fine pearls. After finding a very valuable one, the shop owner sells everything in order to buy that pearl."

"Tell us more," the disciples said.

Jesus told them, "The Kingdom of Heaven is like a **fishing net** that is thrown into a lake and catches all kinds of fish. When the net is full, the fishermen drag it to shore. Then they sit down to see what fish they caught in the net. They keep the good ones and throw the bad ones away.

★ FISHING NET FISHERMEN EITHER USED A CASTING NET, WHICH WAS THROWN OVER THE SIDE OF A BOAT, OR A DRAGNET, WHICH WAS ATTACHED TO TWO BOATS THAT WERE SOME DISTANCE APART.

"That's how it will be at the end of time. Angels will come and separate the evil people from the ones who have done right."

THE WOMAN AT THE WELL

JOHN 4: 3-41

J esus and his disciples were on their way from Judea to Galilee. They took the road through a land called Samaria. The people who lived there came from the families of Jacob, the same as the Jews. But the **Samaritans** and Jews did not get along with one another.

★ SAMARITANS   SAMARITANS WERE THE PEOPLE WHO LIVED IN SAMARIA—THE CENTRAL REGION IN PALESTINE IN BETWEEN GALILEE IN THE NORTH AND JUDEA IN THE SOUTH.

At noon, the disciples went into town to buy some food. Jesus sat near a place called **Jacob's Well** to wait for them.

As he was waiting, a woman came to get water from the well. Jesus asked her to give him a drink.

The woman was surprised. "You are a **Jew**," she said to Jesus. "And I am a Samaritan. Jews will never take anything from Samaritans."

★ JACOB'S WELL   THIS WELL CAN STILL BE SEEN NEAR THE RUINS OF ANCIENT SCHECHEM.

★ JEW   THIS NAME REFERRED TO A PERSON FROM THE SOUTHERN KINGDOM OF JUDAH, OR ANY ISRAELITE WHO LIVED DURING OR AFTER THE EXILE.

"You don't know who I am," Jesus said to her. "If you did, you would ask me for the water that gives life."

"Sir," the woman said, "you don't even have a bucket. Where are you going to get this **life-giving water**?"

Jesus told her, "Everyone who drinks from the water in this well will get thirsty again. But no one who drinks the water I give will ever be thirsty again. It is like a flowing fountain that gives eternal life."

The woman ran back to town. She told the people about Jesus. She said he was the **Messiah**, the Savior they called Christ. Some of the Samaritans went to the well and asked Jesus to stay in their town.

★ LIFE-GIVING WATER JESUS IS SAYING THAT THE WATER HE OFFERS IS LIKE A FOUNTAIN THAT GIVES A NEVER-ENDING SUPPLY OF LIFE.

★ MESSIAH MESSIAH IS A HEBREW WORD THAT MEANS "ANOINTED ONE" OR "CHOSEN ONE"—SOMEONE WHO IS RECOGNIZED AS SPECIAL AND HAS BEEN ANOINTED WITH OIL AS A SIGN.

Jesus stayed for two days. After that, many Samaritans put their faith in Jesus as the woman had. They, too, believed that he was the Savior of the world.

Special Work for the Disciples

LUKE 9: 1–6; MATTHEW 10: 1–15; MARK 6: 7–12

J esus called together his twelve disciples and gave them the power to heal. He wanted them to go out and teach about God's kingdom and heal the sick. They would be special messengers called **apostles.**

★ APOSTLES APOSTLES WERE PEOPLE WHO WERE CHOSEN AND SENT BY CHRIST TO TAKE HIS MESSAGE TO OTHERS. THEY WERE GIVEN SPECIAL RESPONSIBILITY TO LEAD AND TEACH OTHERS ABOUT JESUS.

Jesus told them, "Don't take anything with you. Don't take a traveling bag or food or money, or even a change of clothes.

"When you are welcomed into a home, stay there until you leave that town. If people won't welcome you, leave the town. As you leave, shake the dust from your feet as a warning that God is not pleased with them."

The apostles left and went from village to village, telling the good news and healing people everywhere.

BREAD AND FISH FOR EVERYONE

MATTHEW 14: 13–21; MARK 6: 30–44; LUKE 9: 10–17; JOHN 6: 1–14

When the twelve apostles came back to Galilee, they told Jesus everything they had done and taught. There were so many people around, Jesus said to his friends, "Let's go someplace where we can be alone and get some rest."

They left in a boat for a quiet place they knew about. But many people found out where Jesus was going. They ran to the place where his boat would land. When Jesus got there, he saw a large crowd. Thousands and thousands of men, women, and children were there.

Jesus took pity on the people because they were like sheep without a shepherd. He began teaching them many things and healing the sick.

The people stayed all day. The disciples told Jesus, "The people are getting hungry. Let them leave so they can go to the villages near here and buy something to eat."

Jesus answered, "They do not need to leave. You give them something to eat."

The disciples looked around to see what food they had. The disciple Andrew came back with a small basket. "A boy gave me these five small loaves of **bread** and two **fish**. But what good is that with all these people?"

Jesus told the people to sit down on the grass. He held up the five loaves of bread and two fish. He looked up to Heaven and gave thanks for the food. Then he broke the bread and fish into pieces and gave them to his disciples. The disciples passed food out to the people.

There was enough for everyone! And after everyone was full, there were enough leftovers to fill twelve large baskets.

Jesus had fed five thousand men plus thousands of women and children with just five loaves of bread and two fish.

Jesus Walks on Water

Matthew 14: 22–23; Mark 6: 45–52; John 6: 16–21

Thousands of people who had come to hear Jesus had seen a miracle. They had all been fed with just five loaves of bread and two fish.

Afterward, Jesus told his disciples to go. They got on a boat and started back across the lake.

Jesus sent the crowd of people away. Then he went up on a mountain where he could be alone and pray.

Hours went by, and Jesus was still on the mountain.

By this time, the boat with the disciples was a long way from shore. A strong wind was blowing, and the boat was being tossed around on the waves. The disciples had to row against the wind all night long.

A little while before morning, the disciples saw a figure of a man. He looked like he was walking on the waves! He was coming closer to the boat.

The men were terrified and started screaming. They thought the man was a ghost. But then the man said, "Don't worry! I am Jesus. Don't be afraid."

Jesus reached the boat. He got inside. Right away, the wind died down.

Then the disciples worshipped Jesus. They said, "You really are the Son of God."

The Glory of Jesus

LUKE 9: 28–36; MATTHEW 17: 1–9; MARK 9: 2–10

Jesus knew that God had a special plan for him. Soon his time on earth would be over.

Jesus told his disciples that he would be leaving them. They would carry on his work. The disciples did not understand. They wondered why he was saying these things.

About a week later, Jesus went up to a mountain to pray. He took his disciples Peter, John, and James with him.

After a while, the disciples fell asleep. Jesus went on praying. While he was praying, his face changed. It was shining like the sun. His clothes became a brilliant white.

Suddenly, **Moses** and the prophet **Elijah** were there and speaking with him. They talked about what would happen when Jesus died.

Peter and the other two disciples woke up. They saw how **glorious** Jesus was. They saw Moses and Elijah.

Then the shadow of a cloud passed over them. A voice spoke from the cloud:

"This is My chosen Son. Listen to what he says!"

Peter, John, and James were so afraid when they heard the voice that they

fell flat on the ground. Jesus came over and touched them. He said, "Get up and don't be afraid."

★ MOSES AND ELIJAH   MOSES AND ELIJAH WERE HEBREW PROPHETS WHO LIVED MANY HUNDREDS OF YEARS BEFORE JESUS: ELIJAH LIVED IN ABOUT 800 B.C. AND MOSES LIVED IN ABOUT 1300 B.C.

★ GLORIOUS   HERE JESUS' GLORY IS SHOWN THROUGH THE BRIGHTNESS OF HIS FACE AND CLOTHES. THE CHANGE IS CALLED "TRANSFIGURATION."

When they opened their eyes, they saw only Jesus. He looked the same way he had before.

Then they all began to go down from the mountain. Jesus told the others not to say a word about what had happened. So they didn't say anything until after he had died and risen

THE BLIND MAN SEES

JOHN 9

One day, Jesus and his disciples were walking along a road in Jerusalem. They saw a man who had been blind since he was born. The man had never seen the sun or the moon and stars.

The disciples asked Jesus, "Why was this man born blind? Did he or his parents do something bad that made God punish them?"

Jesus said, "No, they didn't. But because he is blind, you will see God work a miracle for him. As long as I am in the world, I am the light for the world."

Then Jesus spit to wet the ground. He made a ball of mud and rubbed it on the blind man's eyes. He told the man to wash off the mud in **Siloam Pool.**

★ SILOAM POOL THIS POOL IS A RESERVOIR CONSTRUCTED INSIDE THE WALLS OF JERUSALEM. WATER RUNS FROM THE GIHON SPRING ALONG AN UNDERGROUND TUNNEL BUILT BY KING HEZEKIAH.

The man went to the pool and washed the mud off his eyes. When he opened his eyes, he could see!

People asked him what had happened. He told them a man named Jesus had come to him and told him what to do.

"Where is this man now?" they asked him.

"I don't know," he answered. "But he must be a **prophet**, like Elijah and Elisha. He could not do this unless he came from God."

★ PROPHET   A PROPHET IS A PERSON WHO SPEAKS FOR GOD AND WHO RECEIVES AND DELIVERS MESSAGES FOR GOD. THESE MESSAGES COULD BE INTENDED FOR CERTAIN PEOPLE, OR AN ENTIRE NATION.

THE REAL NEIGHBOR

LUKE 10: 25-37

L ove your neighbors as much as you love yourself."
This was one of God's laws that everyone knew.

One day, a teacher in the Temple wanted to test Jesus. He asked, "Who are my neighbors?"

Jesus answered him by telling him this story:

A man was going along a road from Jerusalem to Jericho. Some robbers grabbed him and beat him up. They took everything he had and ran off.

*Soon a **priest** from the Temple came along the same road. He saw the injured man lying there. But the priest did not rush over to help the man. Instead, he crossed the road and went on his way.*

⭐ PRIEST THERE WERE 7,200 PRIESTS AT THE TEMPLE. PRIESTS HAD MANY JOBS, INCLUDING, BLESSING THE PEOPLE, BURNING INCENSE, BLOWING THE RAM'S HORN TO ANNOUNCE FESTIVALS AND THE BEGINNING OF THE SABBATH, TENDING THE TEMPLE LAMP THAT HAD TO BE KEPT LIT ALL THE TIME, AND KEEPING THE HOLY BOOKS.

Later, a **Temple helper** came along. He, too, crossed the road and walked by.

Then a man from Samaria came along the road, riding on a donkey.

The Samaritan stopped and went over to the injured man. He put bandages on the man's wounds. Then he lifted the man onto the donkey and took him to an inn.

★ TEMPLE HELPER   A TEMPLE HELPER'S JOB WOULD HAVE BEEN TO GUARD THE TEMPLE GATES, KEEP ACCOUNT OF THE OFFERINGS, DO BUILDING WORK AND TEMPLE MAINTENANCE, BLOW THE TRUMPET, AND SING DURING WORSHIP.

He took care of the man all night.

The next morning, the good Samaritan gave the innkeeper **two silver coins** and said, "Please look after the man. If you spend more than this on him, I will pay you when I return."

★ TWO SILVER COINS THERE WERE THREE DIFFERENT TYPES OF SILVER COIN IN USE IN ISRAEL AT THAT TIME—THE ROMAN DENARIUS, THE GREEK DRACHMA, AND THE TEMPLE SHEKEL.

When he finished the story, Jesus asked, "Which one of the three people was a real neighbor to the man who was beaten up by the robbers?"

The teacher said, "The one who showed pity."

Jesus said, "Go and do the same!"

MARTHA AND MARY
LUKE 10: 38-41

On the way into the city of Jerusalem, Jesus and his disciples stopped in the village of **Bethany**. A friend named Martha welcomed them into her home.

She went to get something to eat and drink.

★ BETHANY   BETHANY WAS A SMALL VILLAGE SITUATED ABOUT TWO MILES TO THE EAST OF JERUSALEM, ON THE SLOPES OF THE MOUNT OF OLIVES.

In the meantime, her sister, Mary, sat down in front of Jesus. He began to tell her about God and the Kingdom of Heaven. She listened to every word he was saying.

Martha was running around preparing a meal. There were a lot of people to feed. Finally, she went to Jesus and said, "Lord, don't you care that my sister has left me to do all the work by myself? Tell her to come and help me."

Jesus answered, "Martha, Martha! You are worried and upset about so many things, but only one thing really matters. Mary is doing what is best, and it will not be taken away from her."

Healing on the Sabbath
LUKE 13: 10–17, 14: 1–6

Most of the Jewish people in Jesus' time obeyed the **Ten Commandments**, the most important laws that God gave to Moses. The Fifth Commandment says that no one should do any work on the **Sabbath Day**, the day that was set aside for God.

One Sabbath, Jesus was teaching in a synagogue. He saw a woman who had a bad back. She was bent over and could not stand up straight. She had been that way for eighteen years.

★ **TEN COMMANDMENTS**   THE TEN LAWS GIVEN BY GOD TO MOSES AT MOUNT SINAI ARE KNOWN AS THE TEN COMMANDMENTS.

★ **SABBATH DAY**   GOD SAID THE SEVENTH DAY WAS FOR REST AND WORSHIP. THE PHARISEES THOUGHT JESUS WAS WRONG TO HEAL PEOPLE ON THE SABBATH BECAUSE, IN THEIR MINDS, HEALING WAS WORK.

Jesus called her over and said, "You are now well." He placed his hands on her. Right away, she stood up straight and praised God.

The man in charge of the **synagogue** was upset. He said to the people, "There are six days each week when we can work. Come and be healed on one of those days, but not on the Sabbath."

Jesus replied, "Don't you untie your ox or donkey and lead it out for a drink on the Sabbath? This woman has been tied up by pain for eighteen years. Isn't it right to set her free on the Sabbath?"

On another Sabbath, Jesus healed a man whose legs were so swollen, he could hardly walk. Again, the **Temple leader** scolded him.

Jesus said, "If your son falls into a well, wouldn't you pull him out right away, even on the Sabbath?"

Jesus' words made his enemies feel ashamed. But everyone else was happy about the wonderful things he was doing.

★ TEMPLE LEADER ALSO KNOWN AS PHARISEES, THE TEMPLE LEADERS WERE FAMOUS FOR THEIR STRICT OBEDIENCE TO THE LAW. IN ADDITION TO THE LAWS GIVEN TO MOSES, THE PHARISEES ALSO FOLLOWED LOTS OF EXTRA RULES THAT EXPLAINED HOW TO CARRY OUT THE LAW. JESUS SAID THE PHARISEES HAD LOST SIGHT OF WHAT GOD REALLY WANTED.

THE LOST SHEEP
LUKE 15: 1–7, 11–32; MATTHEW 18: 10–11

All kinds of people came to listen to Jesus. He welcomed everybody, even the sinners who did not obey the laws of God.

Some Temple leaders did not think it was right for Jesus to be friendly with such people. They were bad and should be turned away.

So Jesus told them these stories:

*If you have one hundred **sheep**, and one of them gets lost, what will you do? Won't you leave the ninety-nine in the field and go look for the lost sheep?*

And when you find it, you will be so happy! You will carry it home right away. You will call your friends and say, "Let's celebrate! I've found my lost sheep."

★ SHEEP DURING THE DAY, SHEEP GRAZED FREELY AROUND THE WATERING PLACES. AT NIGHT, THE FLOCK WAS GATHERED INTO A FIELD SURROUNDED WITH A STONE WALL.

Jesus said, "In the same way, there is more happiness in Heaven because of one sinner who turns to God than over ninety-ninc good people who don't need to."

Two Sons

LUKE 15: 11–32

J esus also told them another story:

There was once a man who had two sons. The older son stayed at home. He worked hard in the fields.

*The younger son wasn't happy at home. When he was old enough, he took his share of the **family's money** and left home.*

FAMILY'S MONEY   ON THE FATHER'S DEATH, THE YOUNGER SON WOULD HAVE RECEIVED ONE-THIRD OF HIS FATHER'S WEALTH WHILE THE ELDER SON WOULD HAVE RECEIVED TWO-THIRDS.

The young man went to another country and lived a wild life. He didn't care how much money he spent as long as he was having fun. In a few years, the money ran out. The fun stopped. Soon he had nothing to eat.

He went to work for a man. The man sent him out to take care of his **pigs**. The young man would have been glad to eat what the pigs were eating, but no one gave him a thing.

Finally, there was only one thing he could do. He went back home.

★ PIGS TO A JEW, PIGS WERE UNCLEAN ANIMALS. GOD HAD FORBIDDEN JEWS TO EAT PIGS, SO LOOKING AFTER PIGS WAS CONSIDERED A SHAMEFUL JOB.

His father was working out in the fields. He looked up and saw his son all ragged and dirty. He ran to him and hugged and kissed him.

The son told his father he had lived a bad life and was sorry. "I am no longer good enough to be called your son," he said.

But his father was happy to have him back after so many years. He gave him sandals, new clothes, and even a ring for his finger. He got everything ready for a big party to celebrate his return.

This made the older son angry. He had worked hard for his father all the years his brother had been gone. But his father had never done anything special for him.

The father told him, "My son, everything I have is yours. But we should be glad and celebrate! Your brother was dead, but now he is alive. He was lost but has now been found."

TEN MEN ARE HEALED

LUKE 17: 11–19

"Jesus, Master, have pity on us!"

Jesus looked up. He was just going into a village when he heard the cry for help.

He saw ten men standing a little way off. They all had the terrible skin disease called **leprosy**.

★ LEPROSY   LEPROSY WAS THE WORD USED FOR SEVERAL DIFFERENT KINDS OF DISEASES THAT AFFECTED THE SKIN. LEPROSY WAS SERIOUS AND AT THAT TIME THERE WAS NO CURE.

People who had this disease had a very hard life. They were not allowed to be with their families or any other people. No one would touch them because they were afraid of getting the disease.

If, by any chance, the sick people got better, they had to go to a temple and show the **priests** they were well. If the priests said they were cured, they could go back to their families.

When Jesus saw the ten men, he said to them, "Go show yourselves to the priests."

★ PRIESTS It was part of a priest's job to check the healings that had taken place. They also had to see to the purification of the people.

As they were on the way to the priests, the men saw that the sores on their skin were gone! One of the men turned around and ran back to Jesus. He was shouting praises to God. He bowed down at the feet of Jesus and thanked him. The man was from the country of Samaria.

Jesus said, "Ten men were healed. Where are the other nine? This man from another country came back to thank God. Why was he the only one?"

Then Jesus told the man to stand up. "You may go," he said. "Your faith has made you well."

399

Jesus Blesses the Children

MATTHEW 19: 13–15; MARK 10: 13–16; LUKE 18: 15–17

J esus and his disciples stopped in many towns in **Judea**. Just as in Galilee, crowds of people came to see and hear Jesus.

In one place, people brought their children to him. They wanted Jesus to place his hands on the children and bless them.

But the disciples told the people to go away and stop bothering Jesus.

★ JUDEA   JUDEA IS A GREEK WORD FOR THE LAND OF JUDAH, WHICH WAS PART OF THE ROMAN EMPIRE IN NEW TESTAMENT TIMES. IN A LATER PERIOD, JUDEA WAS THE NAME FOR THE SOUTHERN KINGDOM OF ISRAEL. JERUSALEM WAS THE CAPITAL OF THE REGION OF JUDEA. THE PEOPLE WERE CALLED JUDEANS, AND THE WORD "JEW" COMES FROM THIS WORD.

Jesus heard them. He said, "Let the children come to me! Don't try to stop them. People who are like these little children belong to the Kingdom of God.

"I promise you that you cannot get into God's kingdom unless you accept it the way a child does."

Then Jesus took the children in his arms and blessed them by placing his hands on their heads.

A Miracle in Jericho

Mark 10: 46–52; Luke 18: 35–43; Matthew 20: 29–34

A blind man sat near the side of the road to the city of Jericho. He was begging for coins.

Suddenly, the beggar heard the sound of voices. He could tell that a large crowd of people was coming. They sounded excited.

When the voices got closer, the man said, "Tell me, what is happening?"

Someone told him that Jesus from Nazareth was passing by. The blind man shouted, "Jesus! **Son of David**, have pity on me!"

"Shh, shh. Be quiet!" said people in the crowd. But this just made the man shout louder. "Jesus, have pity on me!"

★ **SON OF DAVID** SINCE THE JEWISH PEOPLE EXPECTED THE MESSIAH TO BE FROM THE FAMILY OF KING DAVID, THE MESSIAH WAS OFTEN REFERRED TO AS "SON OF DAVID." WHEN BARTIMAEUS CALLED JESUS THE SON OF DAVID, IT SHOWED THAT HE BELIEVED JESUS WAS THE MESSIAH.

Jesus stopped. He told some people to bring the blind man over to him. The man's name was Bartimaeus. Jesus asked him, "What do you want me to do for you?"

"Lord, I want to see!" Bartimaeus answered.

Jesus told him, "Look and you will see! Your eyes are healed because of your faith."

Now Bartimaeus could see! He saw Jesus and all the people around him. Everyone praised God for this miracle. There was only one thing Bartimaeus wanted to do then: He wanted to join the people and go with Jesus.

And he did.

A Sinner Is Saved

LUKE 19: 1–10

Jesus was walking through the city of Jericho. Many people were crowding around him.

A man named Zacchaeus saw the crowd coming. He was a rich man, but he was not an honest man. He was in charge of collecting **taxes** in Jericho. He asked poor people for more money than they owed and kept the extra money for himself.

★ TAXES   THIS WAS MONEY PAID BY PEOPLE TO THE GOVERNMENT FOR THE COST OF THINGS TO BE BUILT AND SHARED, LIKE ROADS. ZACCHAEUS WAS THE CHIEF TAX COLLECTOR IN JERICHO.

Zacchaeus had heard about Jesus. He was curious to see him. But he was **short** and could not see above the crowd. So he ran ahead and climbed up into a sycamore tree. From there, he could see everything.

Soon, Jesus came walking right under the sycamore tree. He looked up. He said, "Zacchaeus, hurry down! I want to stay with you today."

Zacchaeus was amazed that Jesus would even speak to him. He climbed down from the tree and took Jesus to his house.

People who knew Zacchaeus shook their heads and grumbled. "That man is a cheater and a sinner," they said. "And Jesus is going to his home to eat with him!"

★ SHORT IN JESUS' TIME, THE AVERAGE PALESTINIAN PEASANT WAS ABOUT 5 FEET 1 INCH TALL. SO ZACCHAEUS MUST HAVE BEEN EVEN SHORTER THAN THAT!

Zacchaeus was changed by being with Jesus. Later that day, the rich man stood up and told Jesus that he was going to give half of his money to the poor. And he was going to pay back all the people he had cheated and give them four times as much as he had taken.

Jesus said to Zacchaeus, "I have come to look for and to save people who are lost. Today you and your family have been saved."

At Mary's House

MATTHEW 26: 6–13, MARK 14: 3–9; JOHN 12: 1–8

J esus and his disciples were passing through the village of Bethany. This was where Jesus' friends, the sisters Mary and Martha, lived.

The sisters invited everyone to have dinner at their house.
After the meal, Mary took out a jar of sweet-smelling **perfume**.
It was very expensive.

Mary loved Jesus and wanted to show her love. She got down on her knees and poured the perfume on his feet. Then she wiped Jesus' feet with her long hair, and the room was filled with the sweet smell.

The disciple who was named **Judas Iscariot** didn't like what Mary had done. He said, "That perfume was worth three hundred silver coins! Why didn't you sell it and give the money to the poor?!"

★ PERFUME   This was most probably a sweet-smelling oil that was kept in a sealed jar. It could only be opened by breaking the neck of the jar.

★ JUDAS ISCARIOT   Judas Iscariot was the disciple who betrayed Jesus. Judas was keeper of their money box.

Judas did not really care about the poor. He said this because he was in charge of the moneybag and sometimes would steal from it.

Jesus replied, "Leave Mary alone. She has done a beautiful thing for me. You can give to the poor whenever you want. You will always have them with you, but you won't always have me."

Jesus Comes to Jerusalem

MATTHEW 21: 1–17, MARK 11: 1–11, 15–19; LUKE 19: 28–48; JOHN 12: 12–18

The next day, a large crowd was in Jerusalem for **Passover**. They knew that Jesus was coming for the holiday.

Jesus came riding into Jerusalem on a donkey. The people ran to greet him.

★ PASSOVER   PASSOVER IS A FESTIVAL THAT TAKES PLACE IN MARCH OR APRIL. IT CELEBRATES THE NIGHT GOD FREED HIS PEOPLE FROM SLAVERY IN EGYPT. ON THAT NIGHT, THE ANGEL OF DEATH SWEPT THROUGH THE LAND AND KILLED THE EGYPTIANS' FIRSTBORN SONS, BUT PASSED OVER THE ISRAELITES' HOUSES.

In front of Jesus and behind him people threw **palm branches** on the road and shouted, "Hooray! God bless the one who comes in the name of the Lord. God bless the king of Israel!"

★ PALM BRANCHES   THROWING PALM BRANCHES AND CLOTHES ON THE ROAD WAS A WAY OF WELCOMING AN IMPORTANT PERSON TO THE CITY.

Jesus went to the Temple to look around. He did not like what he saw. The Temple was like a market. People were buying and selling things. There were **money changers** doing business, trading one kind of money for another.

★ MONEY CHANGERS   THE TEMPLE OFFERING HAD TO BE PAID IN SHEKELS, SO PEOPLE NEEDED TO EXCHANGE ROMAN OR GREEK COINS FOR TEMPLE COINS. MANY OF THE MONEY CHANGERS CHEATED THE PEOPLE.

The next day, Jesus came back with his twelve disciples. He began to chase out everyone who was buying and selling. He told them the Temple was a place to worship God, not to do business.

This made some leaders of the Temple very angry. They thought Jesus was a troublemaker. He was becoming too popular. They were afraid the people would turn to Jesus and stop listening to them.

These leaders got together and decided they had to get rid of Jesus. But how? They would have to think of something.

PAYING TAXES

MATTHEW 22: 15-22, MARK 12: 13-17; LUKE 20: 20-26

J esus' enemies had come up with a plan to get rid of Jesus. They sent some men to listen to Jesus teach in the Temple. These men pretended to be friendly. But they tried to trick him into saying something that would get him into trouble with the **Roman leaders**.

So one day, one of the spies asked Jesus, "Teacher, we know that you teach the truth about what God wants people to do. And you treat everyone the same, no matter who they are. Tell us, should we pay taxes to the Roman emperor or not?"

Jesus knew very well what the men were up to. So he said, "Show me a **coin**."

One of the men held up a silver coin.

Jesus asked him, "Whose picture and name is on the coin?"

The man answered, "The emperor Caesar's."

So Jesus said, "**Give Caesar what belongs to him** and give God what belongs to God."

His enemies couldn't find anything wrong with this answer. It surprised them so much that they just walked away.

★ GIVE CAESAR WHAT BELONGS TO HIM   IF JESUS HAD SAID THAT PEOPLE SHOULD NOT PAY TAXES, HIS ENEMIES COULD HAVE ACCUSED HIM OF BEING DISLOYAL TO THE ROMAN RULERS.

THE POOR WOMAN'S FORTUNE

MARK 12: 41–44; LUKE 21: 1–4

One day, Jesus was sitting in the Temple watching people as they put money in the **offering box**. This money was to help pay for the upkeep of the Temple and for things the priests needed. As Jesus watched, he saw all kinds of people giving money. Some rich people put in many silver coins.

Then a poor woman came up to the box. She had **two small coins** in her hand. Together, they were worth only a few pennies. The woman dropped both coins into the box.

★ OFFERING BOX   THERE WERE 13 OFFERING BOXES IN THE COURT OF WOMEN. EACH BOX WAS DESIGNATED TO RECEIVE MONEY FOR A DIFFERENT PURPOSE, SUCH AS WOOD TO BURN THE SACRIFICE, INCENSE, OR OLD VESSELS.

★ TWO SMALL COINS   THESE WERE GREEK COINS MADE OF BRONZE. THEY WERE WORTH A FRACTION OF A ROMAN SILVER DENARIUS.

Jesus called his disciples. He said to them, "Look at this woman. Everyone else gave much more money than she did. But they only gave what they didn't need. This woman has put in more than anyone else. She is very poor, but she gave everything she had."

JESUS THE SERVANT

JOHN 13: 1-20

Jesus and the twelve disciples got together to have the **Passover feast**.

★ PASSOVER FEAST THE MEAL EATEN AT PASSOVER INCLUDES LAMB, BROWN SAUCE, SALT WATER, AND BITTER HERBS. ALL OF THESE ACT AS REMINDERS OF PASSOVER NIGHT. THREE LOAVES OF UNLEAVENED BREAD ARE PUT ON THE TABLE AS A REMINDER THAT THEIR ANCESTORS HAD TO HURRY WHEN THEY LEFT EGYPT AND DID NOT HAVE TIME TO LET THE DOUGH RISE.

After the men started to eat, Jesus stood up. He got a bowl of water and a towel and began to **wash the disciples' feet**.

When he came to the disciple Peter, Peter asked, "**Lord**, are you going to wash my feet?"

Jesus answered, "You don't really know what I am doing, but later you will understand."

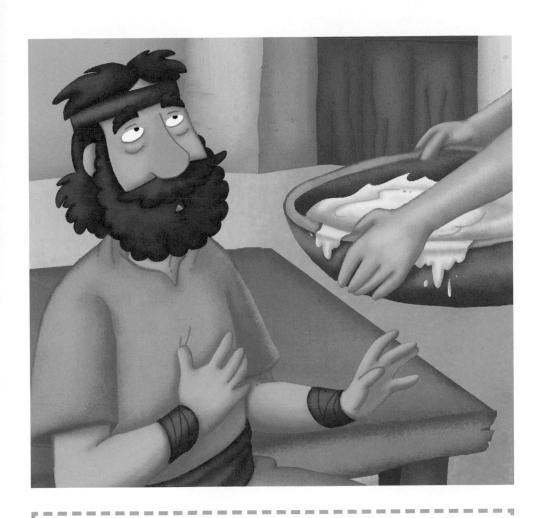

★ WASH THE DISCIPLES' FEET People usually walked barefoot and so their feet got very dirty from the road. A servant would wash the guests' feet when they came in.

★ LORD "Lord" is used as a title to address kings or those in authority. The word in Hebrew is "adonai."

Peter thought Jesus should not be acting like a servant. He said he did not want Jesus to wash his feet.

Jesus told him, "If you don't let me wash your feet, you don't really belong to me."

So Peter let Jesus wash his feet.

When all the disciples' feet had been washed, Jesus spoke to them.

"You call me your teacher and Lord, and you should, because that is who I am.

"I have washed your feet to show you that you should do for one another exactly what I have done for you. You know these things, and God will bless you if you do them."

THE LAST SUPPER

MATTHEW 26: 17–30; MARK 14: 12–26; LUKE 22: 7–23; JOHN 13: 21–30

All twelve of Jesus' disciples were at the Passover feast. The twelve were Peter and his brother Andrew; John and James, sons of Zebedee; Philip; Bartholomew; Thomas; Matthew; James, son of Alphaeus; Thaddaeus; Simon; and Judas Iscariot.

The disciples were all different—some had more faith than others. But they were loyal to Jesus. All but one. Jesus knew this disciple was going to turn against him.

He said, "I tell you for certain that one of you will **betray** me. I will dip this piece of bread in the bowl and give it to the one I am talking about."

Jesus **dipped the bread** and gave it to Judas Iscariot.

★ BETRAY   When you betray someone, you are disloyal to them.

★ DIPPED THE BREAD   Traditonally at meal times, flat bread was used a bit like a spoon and was dipped in the communal dish. As a sign of friendship, the head of the family would choose the best bit and offer it to an important guest.

Judas stood up.

Jesus told him, "Go and do what you must do."

The other disciples watched Judas walk away. They did not know what was going on.

Then Jesus told the others that he would soon be going away from them. It was time for him to die. That was God's plan for him all along.

Then he told them that when he was gone, they must love one another as he has loved them.

The disciples did not want Jesus to leave them. Jesus said, "You are very sad now. But later I will see you, and you will be so happy that no one will be able to change the way you feel."

Jesus took some bread in his hands and blessed it. He picked up a cup of **wine** and gave thanks to God. He shared the bread and wine with the disciples.

★ WINE JEWS DRANK WINE AT SPECIAL MOMENTS DURING THE PASSOVER CELEBRATION TO GIVE THANKS TO THE LORD FOR FREEING HIS PEOPLE FROM SLAVERY. IT SHOWED THAT GOD HAD CHANGED THEIR SADNESS INTO JOY.

"This bread and wine are part of me. Take them as a way of **remembering me**."

Afterward, they sang a hymn and went out to the **Mount of Olives**.

★ REMEMBERING ME   CHRISTIANS CELEBRATE THIS EVENT IN A CEREMONY CALLED HOLY COMMUNION OR THE LORD'S SUPPER.

★ MOUNT OF OLIVES   THIS SMALL BUT IMPORTANT MOUNTAIN WAS SITUATED HALF A MILE EAST OF JERUSALEM, ACROSS FROM THE KIDRON VALLEY.

A DARK FRIDAY

MATTHEW 26: 36–68, 27: 1–2, 11–56;
MARK 14: 32–65, 15: 1–41; LUKE 22: 39–71,
23: 1–49; JOHN 17, 18, 19: 1–37

J esus and his disciples went into a garden on the
Mount of Olives.

Jesus walked into a grove of olive trees to pray. The
others lay down on the ground and went to sleep. They just
could not keep their eyes open.

When Jesus came back, he called to his disciples, "Get up!
Let's go. The time is here for me to be taken away."

Just then, they heard footsteps. A gang of men with clubs and swords came into the garden.

Judas Iscariot was with them. He pointed out Jesus by greeting him with a **kiss**.

The men grabbed Jesus and took him away to jail. One man gave Judas a bag filled with thirty pieces of silver. That was his payment for helping them catch Jesus.

In the morning, Jesus was taken before the Roman governor, **Pontius Pilate**.

Jesus' enemies told the governor, "This man says he is King of the Jews. He is making people turn against the emperor. He should be put to death!"

Pilate asked Jesus, "What do you have to say for yourself? Are you guilty?"

Jesus did not say anything.

The governor was amazed that Jesus did not defend himself. At last, he let his soldiers take Jesus away.

★ KISS   At this time, it was the custom for people to greet each other with a kiss on the cheek.

★ PONTIUS PILATE   Pontius Pilate was the Roman governor of Judea at the time of Jesus' arrest, trial, and crucifixion. He was the one who sentenced Jesus to death.

The soldiers put a red robe on Jesus and a crown of thorns. They made fun of "the king." Then they took the robe off and beat him with whips.

They took him to a place called **Golgotha**. There they nailed him to a cross. This was how the Romans punished people who had committed bad crimes.

★ GOLGOTHA   GOLGOTHA WAS ON THE WEST SIDE OF JERUSALEM, JUST OUTSIDE THE CITY WALLS. IT WAS KNOWN AS THE "PLACE OF THE SKULL," POSSIBLY BECAUSE IT WAS NEAR A LARGE ROCK SHAPED LIKE A SKULL.

At noon, the sky turned dark and stayed that way until three o'clock. At that time, Jesus cried out, "Father, I put myself in your hands!" Then he died.

A crowd of Jesus' friends were watching everything from a distance. After they had seen the terrible sight, they felt brokenhearted and went home.

A Joyful Sunday

Matthew 27: 57–65; 28: 1–10; Mark 15: 42–47, 16: 1–8; Luke 23: 50–56, 24: 1–12; John 19: 38–42, 20: 1–10

One of the people who saw Jesus die on the cross was a rich man named Joseph. He was from the town of Arimathea in Judea.

Joseph was honest and brave. He was a Temple leader, but he did not agree with the ones who had turned Jesus over to the Romans. He had heard Jesus' teachings and believed in what he said.

Now Joseph was sad. He went to Pilate and asked for Jesus' body so he could bury it.

Joseph took the body down from the cross and wrapped it in fine cloth. Then he put it in a **tomb** that had been cut out of solid rock.

★ TOMB A DEAD BODY IS BURIED IN A TOMB. SOMETIMES CAVES WERE USED AS TOMBS. THE CAVE MIGHT BE NATURAL AND ENLARGED, OR SPECIALLY DUG OUT.

The women who had come with Jesus from Galilee were there, too. They watched Joseph place Jesus' body in the tomb and put a large **stone** in front of the cave opening. Then they went to get things ready for the **burial**.

This was Friday, and Saturday was the Sabbath. It was against the Jewish law to bury anyone on the Sabbath, so they had to wait until Sunday.

⭐ STONE The opening of a tomb was often closed by a simple rock or big disc-shaped stone, which could be rolled in a groove across the opening.

⭐ BURIAL Bodies decayed quickly in the hot climate of Judea, so people were usually buried on the day they died.

On Sunday morning, Mary Magdalene, Joanna, Mary the mother of James, and some other women went back to the tomb. To their amazement, the stone had been rolled away. The women went inside. Jesus' body was gone!

Suddenly, two men in shining white clothes stood beside them at the tomb. The women were afraid and fell to their knees.

One of the men said, "Why are you looking in the place of the dead for someone who is alive? Jesus isn't here. He has risen from death."

The women left the tomb. They had to tell the eleven disciples right away.

Most of the disciples didn't believe the story. But Peter ran to the tomb. He looked inside. The only thing he saw was the fine cloth that Joseph of Arimathea had wrapped around the body of Jesus two days before.

JESUS IS ALIVE!
MARK 16; LUKE 24

Two men were on their way out of the city. The men were followers of Jesus. They had believed he was the one who would **save Israel**. Now they were sad.

On the road they met a stranger. The stranger walked with them for a while. They talked about everything that had happened to Jesus. The stranger told them not to be sad. Everything had happened as God had planned.

★ SAVE ISRAEL   THE DISCIPLES, LIKE THE REST OF THE JEWS, WERE LOOKING FOR SOMEONE TO RESCUE THEM FROM ROMAN RULE. JESUS HAD COME TO SAVE ISRAEL—BUT IN A DIFFERENT WAY. HE CAME TO RESCUE PEOPLE FROM THEIR SINS AND HELP THEM BECOME HOLY. HE WAS NOT TRYING TO TAKE OVER THE GOVERNMENT OF ISRAEL.

When the stranger had gone, the men knew that they had been talking to Jesus. They hurried back to Jerusalem to tell his disciples.

The disciples were all together. They listened to the men's story. Could this be true? they asked one another.

As they were talking, they heard another voice speaking to them. They looked up. Jesus was standing there beside them.

The disciples were struck with fear. This must be a ghost, they thought.

Jesus said, "Why are you afraid? Why do you doubt? Look at my hands and feet and see who I am. Touch me. Ghosts don't have flesh and bones as you see I have."

The disciples were so amazed, they could not believe their eyes. Then Jesus asked for **something to eat**. They gave him a piece of baked fish and watched as he ate it.

★ SOMETHING TO EAT   AGAIN, PEOPLE BELIEVED THAT EATING WAS A SIGN THAT SOMEONE WAS ALIVE SINCE GHOSTS DON'T NEED FOOD TO SURVIVE.

Jesus Is Taken to Heaven

MARK 16: 19–20; LUKE 24: 50–53; ACTS 1: 1–11

J esus stayed with his eleven apostles for forty days. He spoke with them about God's kingdom.

One day he said, "Don't leave Jerusalem yet. Wait here. John baptized people with water, but soon you will be **baptized with the Holy Spirit**."

A few days later, one of the apostles asked him, "Lord, are you now going to give Israel its own king again?"

Jesus said that they did not need to know what God had planned or when the events would happen.

★ BAPTIZED WITH THE HOLY SPIRIT   THIS MEANT BEING FILLED WITH GOD'S SPIRIT. THE HOLY SPIRIT WOULD GIVE THE DISCIPLES THE POWER TO TAKE THE GOOD NEWS ABOUT JESUS EVERYWHERE.

"But the Holy Spirit will come upon you and give you power," he told his faithful friends. "Then you will tell everyone about me—people in Jerusalem, in all Judea, in Samaria, and everywhere in the world."

After Jesus had said this, a cloud appeared over their heads. Then, right before their eyes, Jesus was taken up into the cloud. The apostles could not see him, but they kept looking up at the sky as the cloud rose higher and higher.

Suddenly, two men dressed in white clothes were standing beside them. They said to the apostles, "Jesus has been taken to Heaven. But he will come back in the same way that you have seen him go."

THE HOLY SPIRIT

ACTS 2: 1–42

T en days later was a **holiday**. Many of Jesus' followers were all together in one place—the apostles, the women who had come with Jesus from Galilee, and others. There were again twelve apostles. They had chosen the faithful disciple Matthias to take the place of Judas Iscariot, who had betrayed Jesus.

★ HOLIDAY   THIS HOLIDAY WAS PENTECOST—A HARVEST FESTIVAL CELEBRATED IN MAY OR JUNE, FIFTY DAYS AFTER PASSOVER. THE CELEBRATIONS LASTED FOR TWO WEEKS. PILGRIMS CAME TO THE TEMPLE TO THANK GOD FOR HIS LAW AND FOR THE HARVEST. THEY WOULD SING AND BRING LOAVES MADE OF NEW FLOUR.

All at once, the sound of a mighty wind came from Heaven and filled the whole house.

Then they saw flames that looked like tongues moving every which way. A tongue of **fire** came to rest on each one of the followers.

At that moment, all of them were filled with the Holy Spirit. The Holy Spirit gave them the power to speak in different languages.

A large crowd had come to Jerusalem for the holiday. When they heard all the noise, they came to see what was going on. The people had come from **countries** far and near. The people spoke different languages. But they heard Jesus' followers and could understand everything they said.

"What's happening?" they asked. "What does this mean?"

The apostles stood together. Peter spoke to the crowd. He said, "Listen to what I have to say about Jesus of Nazareth. God proved that he sent Jesus to you by having him work miracles and wonders.

★ FIRE   FIRST-CENTURY JEWS WERE FAMILIAR WITH THE IDEA OF GOD'S PRESENCE BEING KNOWN THROUGH FIRE, SUCH AS MOSES SEEING THE BURNING BUSH, AND THE PILLAR OF FIRE LEADING THE ISRAELITES.

★ COUNTRIES   THE VISITORS PROBABLY CAME FROM MODERN-DAY IRAN, TURKEY, EGYPT, AND SAUDI ARABIA.

"Jesus was taken up to sit at the right side of God, and he was given the Holy Spirit. Jesus also gave the Spirit to us, and that is what you are now seeing and hearing."

The people were amazed and afraid. "What should we do?" they asked Peter.

Peter told them, "Turn back to God. Be baptized in the name of Jesus Christ. Then you will be given the Holy Spirit. This promise is for you and your children — for everyone no matter where they live."

Many people in the crowd believed Peter's message. That day, about three thousand men, women, and children were baptized.

A MIRACLE AT THE
BEAUTIFUL GATE
ACTS 3, 4: 1–22

I t was three o'clock in
the afternoon. The
apostle Peter was going into
the Temple in Jerusalem to
pray. Another apostle, John,
was with him.

To go into the Temple,
Peter and John had to pass
through its door, which was
called the **Beautiful Gate**.

Every day at this time, a
man who could not walk sat
by the door. He begged for
money from the people who
were going inside.

The **lame** man saw Peter and John coming up to the door.
He held up his hands and asked them for money.

★ **BEAUTIFUL GATE** THIS WAS PROBABLY A GATE WITHIN THE TEMPLE AREA, LEADING FROM THE COURT OF GENTILES, A LARGER, OUTER COURTYARD AREA, INTO THE COURT OF WOMEN.

★ **LAME** PEOPLE WHO COULD NOT WALK NORMALLY WERE NOT ALLOWED IN THE TEMPLE, BUT COULD SIT BY ITS GATES AND BEG FOR MONEY.

Peter and John looked down and saw the man. Peter said, "Look at us!"

The lame man looked up with a hopeful smile. He thought he was going to get some money. But Peter said, "I don't have any silver or gold. But I will give you what I do have. In the name of Jesus Christ from Nazareth, get up and start walking."

Peter took the man's hand and pulled him up.

At once, the man's feet and ankles became strong. He jumped up. He took some steps. He was walking!

When he was lame, the man was not allowed to go into the Temple. But now he walked through the door with John and Peter. He was walking and jumping and singing praises to God.

The people in the Temple knew that this was the lame man who had just been begging next to the Beautiful Gate. But he was not lame anymore!

Peter told the crowd that the power of Jesus had healed the lame man. The leaders of the Temple did not like what Peter said. But everyone else praised God for the miracle they had just seen.

A New Apostle

ACTS 9: 1–31, 22: 1–16, 26: 9–18

P eter and the other apostles went into cities near Jerusalem to preach. More and more people were baptized in the name of Jesus Christ. They were called **Christians**.

★ CHRISTIANS THE FOLLOWERS OF CHRIST WERE KNOWN AS CHRISTIANS. THE WORD WAS FIRST USED IN ANTIOCH AND MEANS "THE CHRIST-ONES."

But many people thought it was wrong to be a Christian. One of them was a man named Saul. He was an official of the Temple.

Saul didn't want anyone, anywhere to worship Jesus. He was always going into the houses of Christians and taking them off to jail.

Saul heard that Jesus' apostles were preaching in the city of **Damascus**. He had the high priest in the Temple write letters to officials in Damascus. The letters gave Saul the power to

arrest and take to Jerusalem any man or woman in Damascus who believed in Jesus. Then Saul could bring these people to Jerusalem for trial.

★ SAUL   SAUL IS A JEWISH NAME. SAUL LATER CHANGED HIS NAME TO PAUL, WHICH IS A GREEK VERSION OF THE SAME NAME.

★ DAMASCUS   A LARGE NUMBER OF JEWS LIVED IN DAMASCUS. MANY JEWISH CHRISTIANS FLED THERE, TO ESCAPE PERSECUTION. DAMASCUS IS ONE OF THE OLDEST, CONTINUOUSLY INHABITED CITIES IN THE NEAR EAST.

Saul and some other men were on the road to Damascus. They had almost reached the city. Suddenly, a bright light from Heaven flashed all around Saul. The light was so bright, Saul had to close his eyes. He fell to the ground.

A voice said, "Saul! Saul! Why are you so cruel to me?"

"Who are you?" Saul asked.

The voice replied, "I am Jesus. I am the one to whom you are so cruel. Now get up and go into the city. There you will be told what to do."

Saul stood up and opened his eyes. He could not see a thing!

Someone had to take Saul's hand and lead him to Damascus. For three days, Saul was blind.

Then a man came to the house where Saul was staying. The man's name was Ananias. He was a follower of Jesus.

Ananias put his hands on Saul and said, "The Lord Jesus has sent me. He wants you to be able to see and to be filled with the Holy Spirit."

As soon as Ananias stopped speaking, something that looked like fish scales fell from Saul's eyes. He could see again! The Holy Spirit filled him.

Saul stayed with Jesus' followers in Damascus and was baptized. Soon he began to tell everyone that Jesus was the Lord's Way. He became an apostle. After a while, he was called Paul.

PAUL AND SILAS IN PHILIPPI

ACTS 16: 16–40

The apostle Paul took the news about Jesus to places far from Judea. He and his helpers **sailed** in boats on the Mediterranean Sea. They walked along dusty **roads** to cities near the coast.

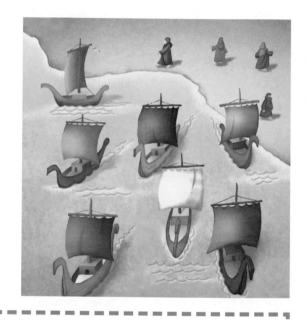

★ **SAILED** For safety reasons, the ships did not sail far from shore, so voyages took a very long time.

★ **ROADS** The Romans are famous for the roads they built, which were often very straight and a lot better than anything that had gone before. A milestone was placed every 1,000 paces.

Paul made many journeys. He baptized thousands of people. But in many towns and cities, Paul got into trouble. The Temple leaders sent people to stir up crowds against him. Often the crowds beat him up and threw him out of town. Sometimes Paul was put in jail.

That's what happened in the town of **Philippi**. Paul was with his friend **Silas**, another apostle.

Some people said that Paul and Silas were telling them to do things they were not allowed to do under the Roman laws.

An angry crowd gathered around Paul and Silas. The two apostles were beaten up and dragged to jail.

In the jail, their feet were chained to heavy blocks of wood. But Paul and Silas were not afraid. They prayed and sang praises to God.

About midnight, the men heard the earth under the jail rumble. The jail began to shake. It was an earthquake!

★ PHILIPPI   PHILIPPI WAS A CITY IN THE ROMAN PROVINCE OF MACEDONIA, IN MODERN-DAY NORTHERN GREECE. AT THAT TIME, IT WAS A ROMAN COLONY AND A BUSY TRADING PLACE.

★ SILAS   SILAS WAS A JEWISH CHRISTIAN AND LEADER OF THE CHURCH AT JERUSALEM. HE WAS ALSO KNOWN AS SILVANUS.

The shaking got stronger and stronger. Suddenly, the doors opened and the chains fell away.

Paul and Silas could have walked right out. But they didn't.

The next morning, some guards came to the jail. They were surprised to see that Paul and Silas were still there. The guards told the two apostles that they were free to go.

But Paul said, "We are Roman citizens. The officials in this town let us be beaten and put into jail without a trial. Now they want to send us away in secret. No, they cannot! They will have to come here themselves and let us out."

Roman citizens had special rights, and the town officials didn't want to get into trouble. So they went to the jail. They told Paul and Silas they were sorry for what had happened and led them out of jail.

Afterward, Paul and Silas left Philippi and went to other towns. Nothing could stop them from preaching and telling the world about Jesus.

★ ROMAN CITIZENS   ROMAN CITIZENS WERE TREATED BETTER THAN OTHER CITIZENS. THEY HAD SPECIAL RIGHTS AND PRIVILEGES UNDER THE LAW. PAUL MAY HAVE HAD THIS HONOR PASSED ON TO HIM BY AN ANCESTOR WHO HAD BEEN REWARDED FOR DISTINGUISHED SERVICE.

A NEW WORLD

REVELATION 1, 22: 8 – 21

In time, thousands of people became Christians. There were Christians in many parts of the world, even in the city of **Rome**.

But most people still believed in Roman gods and goddesses. Then the government of Rome told the people that the emperor was a god, too. Everyone had to **worship** him.

★ ROME ROME WAS AN IMPORTANT CITY IN ITALY AND CAPITAL OF THE ROMAN EMPIRE IN NEW TESTAMENT TIMES. ROME HAD OVER A MILLION CITIZENS WHEN JESUS LIVED ON EARTH.

★ WORSHIP WHEN YOU WORSHIP SOMEONE, YOU SERVE, REVERE, HONOR, OR PRAISE THEM AS MASTER, OR YOU ARE DEVOTED TO THEM.

The Christians went on worshipping God and Jesus, the Son of God. They would not worship the emperor even though it meant they could be punished.

One Christian leader named John would not stop teaching about Jesus. He was sent far away to an **island**.

★ ISLAND THIS WAS PATMOS, A ROCKY, MOUNTAINOUS ISLAND OFF THE COAST OF MODERN-DAY TURKEY. PEOPLE WHO CRITICIZED THE ROMAN EMPEROR WERE SOMETIMES SENT THERE AS A PUNISHMENT.

One Sunday, John felt the Holy Spirit fill his mind. It was like being in a dream that seemed real.

In the dream, John heard a loud voice that sounded like a trumpet. He turned to see who was speaking.

John saw Jesus. He was wearing a long robe with a gold cloth wrapped around his chest. He was shining as bright as the sun.

John fell at his feet. But Jesus put his right hand on John and told him, "Don't be afraid. I am the living one. I died, but now I live forevermore.

"I am coming soon! And when I come, I will reward everyone for what they have done.

"God will bless all who have done right. For them there will be no more death, suffering, crying, or pain.

"But those who have done evil will be thrown into a lake of burning fire."

Jesus showed John many **visions** of the future. Later, John wrote everything down in a book.

At the end of the book he wrote, "So, Lord Jesus, please come soon! I pray that the Lord Jesus will be kind to all of you."

★ VISIONS   A VISION IS A PROPHECY OR REVELATION IN WHICH A PERSON SEES SOMETHING THAT GOD WANTS HIM OR HER TO SEE. MANY OF THE PROPHETS RECEIVED THEIR MESSAGES THROUGH VISIONS.

INTRODUCTION
THESE PARENT PAGES ARE FOR YOU!

R ecent studies point out that parents are still the most influential people in their children's lives. These Parent Pages are intended to help you, the best role models for your children, to be equipped and motivated to share your faith through reading the Bible and discussing its stories in a friendly and informal way.

It will be an enjoyable experience for you and for them. It will be fun! It will bring you closer together. It will help you to laugh, learn, and love together.

Happy reading! Happy sharing!
– Rich Bimler

PARENTS AND CHILDREN

TEACHING FORGIVENESS

(GENESIS 31-33)

Forgiveness is God's gift to all people. In the Bible story, Jacob was worried that Esau would not forgive him. He tried to do nice things for his brother so that he might forgive and like him again. But what a great feeling it was for Jacob to find out that Esau had already forgiven him. And that's just how forgiveness works with us. Jesus continues to forgive us, just the way we are, always . . . and that's a long time!

After reading the Genesis 31–33 story about Jacob and Esau, share with your family a time when you were forgiven by one of your parents or other family members when you were young.

Ask your children to share a time when they were forgiven by you, and also a time when they felt they were not forgiven by you.

The key to our living and sharing forgiveness with others is that we do it not because we are nice or that the other person deserves it, but rather because God through Jesus has forgiven us, especially when we do not deserve it.

Tell your children, right now, that you need their forgiveness when you are not as loving or caring as you could be. Tell them of a time when you were sorry for your actions toward them, and ask them to say, "I forgive you, Dad (Mom)." Now ask them to say something like, "Mom (Dad), please forgive me for the time I . . . (have them share a time when they did something wrong).

Life is for giving . . . and forgiving!

RESURRECTION RESOURCES

(MATTHEW 28)

The Resurrection of Jesus is the key to our faith.

Ask your children to think of things that grow around them (flowers, grass, babies, moths). Help them think of other items familiar to them. A seed looks dead, but it blossoms into a beautiful flower. A caterpillar looks dull, but it becomes a beautiful butterfly . . . and on and on and on!

Jesus died on Good Friday, and it looked as though his life was over. But Jesus' Resurrection proves that he is alive now, today. Reread Matthew 28.

Ask your family members how they would have felt if they had been at the tomb on Easter Sunday. Would they have been happy, sad, surprised, or afraid?

In the coming days, put together an Easter surprise for your family . . . even if it is not Easter! Get paper bags for each of them. Place in the bags things that remind you of resurrection . . . a butterfly picture, a seed, a balloon, a picture of Jesus, a flower. Give these Easter bags to your family and encourage them to add other items that remind them of Jesus' Resurrection.

WE ARE BLESSED

(MATTHEW 19)

R ead Matthew 19 with your family. Children were, and are, a priority for Jesus. Share with your family the fact that the Lord continues to love all children through their parents and other adults.

Some of the adults in this story did not think children were that important. That is true today also. Discuss together some of the adults in your lives who are friendly and helpful to you and also some who may not always be that encouraging and helpful to little ones.

Sing or say together, "Jesus loves the little children, all the children in the world; red and yellow, black and white, they are precious in his sight; Jesus loves the little children of the world."

Thank your family for being your family. Tell them that you love them and that they are special blessings to you. And then say to one another, "You are a real blessing to me!"

We are blessed by the Lord to be blessings to others!

TELL JESUS' STORY

(LUKE 2: 8-14)

This is one of the greatest stories in the Bible. An angel appeared to the shepherds and announced that Jesus was being born. The shepherds were very afraid, but the angel said, "Don't be afraid! I bring you good news."

The Lord comes to us each day also. He comes through words and actions and people, and even through your family. And He allows us to be like the angel and tell the story of Jesus.

Tell your family the following story: A girl was asked to be the angel in the church Christmas program. She carefully memorized her lines — "Don't be afraid, I have great news that will bring joy to you." But when the time came for her to speak, she became afraid and could not remember the exact words. But she did know the meaning of them. So she shouted out, "Hey, don't worry. Do I have good news for you!"

It does not matter how we tell the story, or what words we use. Jesus was born to love, forgive, and bless all of us each day.

Close your time together by saying to one another, "Don't be afraid, Jesus is with us."

Parent Page 5
Make People Well
(Luke 4)

Read Luke 4 as a family. This is one of many stories of how Jesus went around healing people.

Ask the question "How does Jesus heal people?" There are many ways that he continues to bring health to people of all ages. He does it through nurses and doctors when they care for us. He does it through grandparents and other older adults when they stay with young ones. He certainly does it through parents when they love and listen and hug their children.

Jesus does not only heal people physically, but he heals them in mind, body, and spirit. People are really healed when they know that God loves and forgives them, whether or not they are sick or disabled in some way.

Jesus continues to heal people — right now, today — through each of us. He does this when we love and care for one another.

SERVING OTHERS

(JOHN 13)

R ead the Bible story in John 13. Washing feet does not sound like something that everyone would love to do, right? But ask your children to think of a time when you did wash their feet, or bandaged a cut hand, or helped clean their room, or washed their dirty faces, or washed their clothes. It's sort of the same thing.

Jesus washed his disciples' feet to show that he was a special helper to them. And he sends people into our lives to help us when we cannot do things by ourselves, like parents and teachers and grandparents.

He also told this story to show us that we are all helpers to people around us. Because Jesus loves and serves us, we can now love and serve other people.

Discuss people in your family and neighborhood who need help. How can you help them? What can you do for someone this week, even if he did not ask for help? Maybe you could walk someone's dog or take out the trash for her. Maybe a nice hug would make him feel better. Help doesn't have to be a big thing; it can be something quite simple.

Close your discussion by thanking Jesus for sending people into our lives who help us, so that we can help other people.

WE ARE LOVED

(LUKE 15: 11-32)

The joy of family living is to know that we are loved always, even when we do not deserve it. That's the heart of every action and reaction in a family. When all is said and done, and when things are wrongly said and not done . . . we are still loved by our family and by the Lord! And even when we fail to say kind words or do kind things, God's love is always with us.

What a gift of love we have to share.

That's what this story about family says to us today. A young boy leaves home and gets mixed up in worldly things. He returns home and finds that his brother is upset because their father accepts and continues to love his younger son. It happens in one way or another in every family.

Talk to your family today about God's love for all people. The best way to love is to say and show it each day. Within a family, even when love is not always shared, there still is love because of Jesus living in us!

FACING THE FEARS OF LIFE

(LUKE 8)

Ask your family the question "Have you ever been afraid of something?" Have each person share a story of when he or she was afraid, starting with you.

Everyone, young and old, has been afraid of something. It is human nature to fear the unknown, sickness, family problems, the future, and so on, just like the disciples in the boat. Read Luke 8 together. Notice how scared these people were, even when Jesus was in the boat with them.

Point out that being afraid of something is not due to a lack of faith. Jesus is always with us, in our "boat of life," even though we might sometimes think he is sleeping and not paying attention to us. Jesus is the one who can calm the storms in our lives and quiet the winds of worry around us, but he does it on his timetable.

Parents bring calm and security to their children, especially when family members are worried and upset about thunder and lightning, tomorrow's test, the fear of being bullied, or even rejection.

It is helpful for parents to assure their children of God's presence, especially during scary times, by holding them, asking them what bothers them, and telling them that God is near and cares for them.

In one sense, when we calm and love and hold our children, they are being touched with Jesus' healing hand of acceptance and love. Listen closely to signs and sounds of fear in your children's lives. Reach out to them, as Jesus does with all of us. Remind your family often what the angels say throughout the Bible, "Don't be afraid . . . I am with you!"

WE ARE HOPE-FILLED!

(LUKE 2)

R ead Luke 2 as a family. This wonderful story can be read and shared anytime during the year. It is filled with so much hope for everyone, young and old. And it sounds even better when it is read by someone who is surrounded by family members.

Talk about how each of you would have felt to be there when Jesus was born. What would you have said or done? Isn't it amazing that Jesus was born in a quiet little place like Bethlehem, and in a barn with animals and shepherds? This fact certainly helps us to know that Jesus came for all people: young and old, rich and poor, black and white.

Tell this story of a little boy who was playing the part of the innkeeper in the Sunday school Christmas play. When asked by Joseph if he had room in the inn, the little boy got so excited about Jesus' birth that he forgot his lines and said, "Sure, come on in!"

The Christmas story gives us hope, even when we do not feel hopeful.

Hope is knowing that even when there is no hope . . . there's hope in the Lord!

Remind your children that Jesus came to give all people hope. The Christmas story says it all: "There in Bethlehem . . . Jesus was born!" And he continues to be born in us each day as we live and share this hope of God's love and forgiveness for all of us.

Ask your family to watch for hopeful things that will remind them of Jesus' birth . . . a newborn baby, a kind word from a friend, a chance to help someone out. Close your discussion by reading the Luke 2 story again.

Celebrate hope in the Lord and have a Merry Christmas — every day!

SHARE YOUR GIFTS

(MATTHEW 2)

Begin your time together with a prayer, thanking the Lord for all of the gifts He has given to each of you. Take the time for each person to thank the Lord for one gift that He has given to him or her (i.e., "Thanks, Lord, for giving my mom the gift of listening, and my dad the gift of laughter," etc.).

Read Matthew 2 and talk about what gifts each of you would have brought to Jesus to celebrate his birth. What is your favorite gift that the Lord has given to you? Is it music, or listening, or athletics, or writing, or helping others? Make a list of these gifts and display them for the next week.

All of us have been given so many abilities and gifts. Everybody has been blessed with many things that he or she can do well, like cooking, or organizing, or caring, or fixing things, or telling stories. The Wise Men brought expensive gifts to Jesus. The gifts we share with others are also very valuable because they help other people, just like Jesus did. When we listen to Mom, that is a gift we are giving back to the Lord.

When we forgive our children, that is indeed a great gift. When we take care of our little brother, that is a gift we are offering to Jesus.

Discuss with your family the fact that often we concentrate on the abilities we do not have, the mistakes we make, the limitations we all have. Isn't it great that none of us can do everything well? Because of that, we need to rely on one another and help others use the gifts the Lord has given to them.

The first Wise Men gave gifts to Jesus, and now Jesus makes it possible for us to give gifts to those around us, starting with our own family.

End your discussion by telling how each of you plans to use some special gift to help someone else during the coming week. Say together, "Thank You, Lord, for all of the gifts You have given to us."

REDEEMED
(MATTHEW 26-27)

B egin with this prayer: "Jesus, thank you for dying on the cross for us. Thank you for giving up your life so that we can have new life in you. Amen."

Sharing with your family the fact that Jesus had to die to redeem each of us is a powerful message of love and forgiveness. Because of our sins, God sent Jesus into the world to give up his life so that we could have new life! Ask your children how they feel about Jesus having to die for us. (Answers might be sad, thankful, grateful, confused, or guilty.) Remind your family that Jesus died so that we could live forever, now and in Heaven.

Ask if anyone knows why we call the day Jesus died Good Friday. Share the fact that we call the day Jesus died "Good" because we know that after three days Jesus rose from death and the grave, and that is such "good" news for all of us.

Live this day knowing that the life Jesus lived and the death he died qualify us to receive the life he lived. And the best thing parents can do for their children is to know and then to share the fact that we all have been redeemed by Jesus' death on the cross.

Share this Good News in all that you do today and every day.

LOVE OTHERS

(LUKE 10)

Ask your children to discuss your neighbors. Who are they? What do you like about them? How do they help you and your family to enjoy life more? If one of them needed your help, would you give it? Why or why not? God puts people into our lives for us to help and for us to celebrate. We love others because Jesus loves us. Today is a good day to thank the Lord for your neighbors, even those who sometimes upset you or disappoint you. Make the point to your family that neighbors are not only there to help you, but they are also there to be helped, to be accepted, and to be forgiven.

Luke 10 is a great story about how the Lord encourages us to help everyone, beginning with our family and our neighbors. It is certainly easier to help those whom we like and those who are "like us." But the Lord also asks us to help those whom we do not especially like, or even those whom we do not know.

Decide as a family to do something helpful for someone in your neighborhood or anywhere in the whole world.

Maybe you could bring a food basket to a poor family, or sponsor a child in South America, or go as a family to a homeless shelter and serve food for a weekend. There is so much to do to help your "neighbors" throughout the world. The family that together helps others feels happier and healthier together.

Today Jesus says to you and to your family, "Go and do the same."

PARENT PAGE 13
FRIENDS
(1 SAMUEL 18-19)

Ask your children to name their best friends. Why did they think of these people? Discuss the reasons. Have a prayer thanking the Lord for all of the people mentioned, saying something like, "Lord, thank you for our friends. Thank you for putting people in our lives who know us and love us. Thanks for being our friend, Jesus. Amen."

Friends are gifts from the Lord. In the story of David and Jonathan, in I Samuel 18–19, we see how friendship develops and how important it is to have close friends. Share as a family some stories of how friends helped each of you.

To have a friend we all need to be a friend. David and Jonathan were friends to each other because they decided to help each other when problems arose and when each of them needed help and support.

What are some things you can do for your best friend today? What is it that you think he or she needs from you today? And what do you need from your best friend?

David and Jonathan were good friends because they both loved God and were loved by Him. Thank God today for all of your friends, and especially for our mutual friend, Jesus.

Living by the Promise
(Genesis 6-9)

The story of Noah and the flood is all about God's promise to us. God has promised us that He will love us and be faithful to us all the time.

Share with your children the power and joy of knowing that we have a loving God who will never leave us. His promise is ours even when we do not act like it, or look like it, or feel like it.

Ask your family members to share a time when they made a promise to someone or when someone promised them something. Ask how often your children hear or make the statement "I promise" (to clean my room, take out the garbage, do my homework, play catch with you, take you to a ball game). It is easy to make promises but often hard to follow through on them.

The story of Noah says that even when we make or break our promises to people, God always keeps His promises to love and forgive us. And that makes us special because we know we always have a loving God.

Ask if anyone would like to have been Noah or anyone else on the ark. It must have been an exciting voyage but filled with doubt and questions about the outcome.

Assure your children that even when they break promises or do not do things that they should, God's love is always there, just like in Noah's life.

Isn't it a joy to know that even when we forget who we are, we can remember the promise of the rainbow and remember God's love for us?

WONDERING ABOUT WONDER
(GENESIS 1-2)

R ead Genesis 1-2 as a family. Isn't it a wonder-filled story about the power and creation of God? What day would each of them have liked to experience when God was creating the world? How about the first day, when light was made; or the fifth day, when the fish

and the birds were created? Have fun thinking and sharing how God created everything. Do you think He got tired?

Did He ever make a mistake? Is there something you wish He would have created instead of . . . ?

Now take a look at your own body — big or small, old or young. Each of you is a wonder-filled part of God's creation also.

Have your children look around and select something that God has made that they especially like and enjoy. Encourage them to be creative — after all, they are creatures of the Creator. Maybe they would pick a bottle of water, a special flower, a rock, the dog, the TV, a favorite picture of the mountains. Ask each person to share why he or she picked that item. Enjoy the discussion — and say "Wow" after each person shares his or her special item.

Throughout the day, encourage your family to look at specific parts of God's creation and thank the Lord for creating it. Encourage them to say "Wow" to themselves or to others as they do this.

Thank God by praying, "Lord, thanks for creating everything in life, including my family . . . and also me. Help me to enjoy all of your gifts that you have created. And help me to say 'Wow' each day to you, in Jesus' name. Amen."

WORSHIP

(1 KINGS 8)

Read the majestic story of King Solomon's Temple. Can you imagine a building taking so long to complete? Have your family members draw a picture of a church. How big would they make it? What would they put into it?

A church building is a place where people go to worship the Lord. It may be a very big structure or it may be a very small building. It might hold 3,000 people, or it might be large enough for only fifty people. The size isn't as important as the people who come to these buildings to worship God and to thank Him for His love and forgiveness in Jesus Christ.

A church building is very important for children and parents because it gives all of us a chance to come together to pray, to sing, to read the Bible, and to share how the Lord always loves us. It is also important to worship with other people who love the Lord because it helps us to be encouraged and to grow in the faith.

Point out that in I Kings 8, Solomon, a very wise person, shared his faith by saying, "Lord, no other god in heaven or earth is like You!"

That is his statement of faith. And that is why we worship: to share our faith in the Lord.

Talk about your favorite parts of a worship service. Is it the singing, or the praying, or the message . . . or maybe even the doughnuts after the church service?

The Bible also points out that we can worship God at any time and in any place. We do not have to be in a church building to thank and praise Him. Isn't it a joy to be able to pray at home when we go to bed, or to sing "Jesus Loves Me" during the day?

In your prayers today, thank the Lord for church buildings, where we can go to worship. Thank the Lord for clergy and teachers, who are blessings to you. And especially thank the Lord for the opportunities your family has to pray and sing and study the Bible whenever you want to and wherever you are.

Close your family discussion by saying, "Thank You, Lord, for being our God. Thank You for helping us to worship You anytime of day or night. In Jesus' name, amen."

PRAY

(MATTHEW 6: 9-13)

Prayer is a gift from the Lord that is always available to us. The Lord's Prayer in Matthew 6: 9–13 is the most often-repeated prayer by Christians throughout the world because it covers life and needs and hopes. It strongly affirms that our heavenly Father is the Lord of us and all of life.

As a family, read the Lord's Prayer and stop at the end of each sentence. Ask family members to think of events that happened in their lives today that fit in with each thought. We honor God by not using His name carelessly or without thought. Think of all the gifts that God has provided you this day. Who have we forgiven today? What were we tempted to do today? How did the Lord protect us from evil today?

Remind your children that this prayer is the Lord's Prayer and that prayer helps us to remember that the Lord is with us always and guards and protects us in all things.

Remind the family also that prayer is not the way we demand or insist that God give us what we want. Rather, it is a way that God uses to draw us closer to Him and to know that He is the source of all good things in life.

Pray the Lord's Prayer every day as a family. The Lord is always with us through prayer.

You may also want to say the following prayer as a family before meals or at any time: "Come, Lord Jesus, be our guest, and let these gifts to us be blessed. And may there be a goodly share on every table everywhere. Amen."

TRUST

(EXODUS 16-17)

Read the story of Moses and the Israelites in the desert. Ask your children how they would have felt if they were with Moses and the food was running out. Ask each person to shout out a word that would describe how he or she might have been feeling, such as hungry, sad, scared, forgotten, or tricked.

This is a powerful lesson about trust. We all need people around us to trust. Ask your family members whom they trust — parents, friends, pastors, teachers, or neighbors? How do you know when you can trust someone?

Do this experiment. Have a child stand on a chair, face one of his parents, close his eyes, then jump toward the parent. Have others try it also. Did he jump? Was he scared? Why did he, or why didn't he, jump?

It has to do with trust. If we trust someone, we will believe in that person and will be willing to "jump" into things because we trust that we will be safe.

This is exactly what happened in Exodus. People had trusted Moses, but then they started to doubt him when they were running out of food and water. But when the Lord provided them with water at Horeb, at the big rock, and when food was once again available, they knew they could trust God because He did what He had said He would do. That's trust.

Family members can trust one another but sometimes we let one another down also. We have friends we trust, but they, too, can disappoint us. God is the only One who can be trusted and He never lets us down. He has told us and has shown us that He can be trusted. Today, thank the Lord for His love and forgiveness. Thank Him because He is a God who can be trusted, because He is always with us, providing us with all that we need.

To close your sharing, pray, "Lord, we thank You that You can be trusted. Help us to be people whom others can trust also. Forgive us when we are not trustworthy. We trust You, Lord. Amen."

Encourage one another to live today trusting God's promises of love and joy and peace in our lives.

GIVE THANKS!

(LUKE 17)

Enjoy sharing with your children by making a big sign that reads T-H-A-N-K-S. Ask every person to think of things that they are thankful for, beginning with the letters T-H-A-N-K-S.

Make a list of these words and display them for the next few days. This is a great reminder of how we are thankful for all the gifts God gives to us.

Now read the Luke 17 story about ten people who were healed by Jesus and how only one of them took the time to say thanks. Discuss why you think the other nine didn't return to thank the Lord. Are we like those nine, or like the one who gave thanks? Comment that all of God's people are both like the nine and also the one who thanked the Lord. The good news is that God continues to love all people, those who thank Him regularly and those who sometimes forget to thank Him.

But it is so much fun to give thanks to God for all that He gives us. By doing so, we remember that God is the giver of all gifts and that He has given us life and friends and health to share with others.

Think of ways that each of your family members can give thanks to God for the big and little gifts in life. How does someone who is a good singer give thanks to God? By singing. How does a teacher give thanks? By teaching well. How does a loving parent give thanks? By loving her children. Remind one another that we thank the Lord by using the gifts God has given us and by thanking Him through our prayers.

Tell the story about the father who gave each of his children five candy bars and asked what they would do with them. One child said he would eat them all. One said she would give them all away because she didn't like that type of candy bar. Another one said that she would say thanks to her dad, eat one of them, and give the rest away to those who needed something to eat. And that's what saying thanks is all about in the Bible. We are to thank the Lord for our gifts, use the gifts that He has given to us, and share the gifts with others around us.

Close your sharing by giving each person something to use and to share with someone else. Candy bars, stickers, coins, a bookmark . . . be creative! Close with a prayer, asking each person to pray for something that starts with a T, an H, an A, an N, a K, and an S.

STICK TOGETHER

(RUTH 1-4)

I t's fun to "stick together" through good times and bad times. That is one purpose of a family, to always be available and present to love and care for family members even when it is hard and takes a lot of time.

That is one of the key lessons in Ruth 1–4, as Naomi and Ruth "stick together" in good times and bad times.

Discuss how other things stick together, like magnets, or Velcro. Can your family think of other examples? Emphasize that God provides His people with the ability to "stick together" through our daily journeys and experiences. Share some examples of how your family has stuck together in recent days.

But the good news is that the Lord loves each of us, even when we do not always agree and stick together. He encourages us to be like Naomi and Ruth, but He also forgives us when things do not work out. This Bible story is a great example of how God provides for family and friends to support and encourage one another, through our good days and also our bad days.

To close, think of people in your family's life who have stuck together and who have supported your family.

Promise each family member that you will stick with him or her through the coming week. Remember to thank Naomi and Ruth for being great models of friendship and hope for each of us.

THE LORD'S PRAYER

Our Father in Heaven,
help us to honor Your name.
Come and set up Your kingdom,
so that everyone on earth will obey You,
as You are obeyed in Heaven.
Give us our food for today.
Forgive us for doing wrong,
as we forgive others.
Keep us from being tempted
and protect us from evil.

FAVORITE TEACHINGS OF JESUS

"Make your light shine, so that others will see the good that you do."
Matthew 5

"Ask and you will receive, search and you will find, knock and the door will be opened for you."
Matthew 7

"Treat others as you want them to treat you."
Matthew 7

"You have only one Lord and God. You must love Him with all your heart, soul, mind, and strength. The second most important commandment says, 'Love others as much as you love yourself.' No other commandment is more important than these."
Mark 12

"Your heart will always be where your treasure is."
Luke 12

"God loved the people of this world so much that He gave His only son, so that everyone who has faith in him will have eternal life."
John 3

"I am the way, the truth, and the life. Without me, no one can go to the Father."
John 16